# Global Perspectives on Research Ethics and Scholarly Integrity:

## Proceedings of the 2008 Strategic Leaders Global Summit on Graduate Education

**August 31-September 2, 2008**
**Florence, Italy**

**COUNCIL OF GRADUATE SCHOOLS**

# Global Perspectives on Research Ethics and Scholarly Integrity: Proceedings of the 2008 Strategic Leaders Global Summit on Graduate Education

ISBN-13: 978-1-933042-23-7
ISBN-10: 1-933042-23-0

10 9 8 7 6 5 4 3 2 1          10 09 08

# TABLE OF CONTENTS

## CONTENTS

CONTENTS

# FOREWORD

The 2008 Strategic Leaders Summit in Florence, Italy, addressed one of the most challenging, but also one of the most important, topics in graduate education today. Scholarly Integrity is an issue that takes on new dimensions in a global context, raising questions that require a greater degree of collaborative work among leaders in graduate education. New global partnerships in research and education, from joint and dual degree programs to international research projects, challenge us to clarify the principles that govern ethical research in our own domestic contexts, and to work together to build ethical principles that unite the ever-growing number of projects that transcend national borders. While the participants in this year's Global Summit recognized that culture, along with national priorities, shape our views on these topics, all recognized the value of working to learn from one another. This discussion accomplished an important first step toward building a shared understanding of the ethical issues affecting graduate students, faculty, and university leaders worldwide.

Debra W. Stewart
President
Council of Graduate Schools

# ACKNOWLEDGMENTS

I n addition to thanking each of the participants at the Florence meeting for their thoughtfully prepared contributions to this volume, I would like to acknowledge the CGS staff members who helped make this publication possible: Daniel Denecke and Eleanor Babco, who played a key role in conceptualizing and organizing the meeting; Julia Kent, who edited the manuscript; and Emily Esman, who helped prepare the final manuscript for print.

The Florence Global Summit was made possible with a generous gift from ProQuest, the official publisher of U.S. dissertations. On behalf of the Council of Graduate Schools, I would like to thank them for their interest in the timely and important topic of this meeting and for their ongoing support of graduate education and research.

Debra W. Stewart
President
Council of Graduate Schools

# I. INTRODUCTION: SCHOLARLY INTEGRITY AND RESEARCH ETHICS IN A GLOBAL CONTEXT

The 2008 Strategic Leaders Summit built upon the successes of the first Strategic Leaders Global Summit held in Banff, Canada, in 2007. At the first summit, participants worked to identify a set of principles to guide and strengthen international collaboration and advance graduate education globally. One of the key outcomes to emerge from that conference was a plan for a more extended series of meetings focusing on best practices in global issues related to graduate education. In our discussions with several of our international partners, the topic of scholarly integrity and research ethics clearly emerged at the top of the agenda as the best theme for the first of these best practice meetings, and our 2008 meeting was given the title "Scholarly Integrity and Research Ethics in a Global Context." We are pleased to publish the results of that summit here, as part of a new series, *Global Perspectives on Graduate Education*.

One of the key findings of the global summits was that the old axiom, "where you stand depends on where you sit" holds true both geographically and nationally. Both the context and the content shape discussions about the structure and the implementation of best practices in graduate education. But it was also clear that while our solutions to challenges are not always universal, many of the challenges themselves are shared. In this spirit, the 2008 Global Summit sought to

1. Identify specific institutional and inter-institutional ethics and integrity issues on which we could work commonly
2. Enhance our understanding about the specific structure and strategies in place in different countries and regions of the world to address the most pressing issues of scholarly integrity and research ethics
3. Share experiences with barriers to change, as well as with opportunities for creative solutions and collaborative research and educational programs
4. Register the collective hopes and aspirations of the group assembled here for international collaboration on scholarly integrity

The purpose of the 2008 summit in Florence was to share national, regional, and comparative perspectives on scholarly integrity and research ethics in a global context and to identify possible areas for future collaboration. This year we were most pleased to include participants from countries represented at the 2007 meeting—Canada, the United Kingdom, Australia, China, and the United States—but also to expand participation from last year's meeting to include Africa, Hong Kong, China, the Czech Republic, Germany and Italy.

Clearly, such broad global participation allowed us to explore a wide array of important topics and issues. At the Banff Summit we learned that it is best to begin with presentations on the current terrain of research ethics and training in each country represented, so issues of national policy framework differences and differences in terminology can be addressed and clarified up front. The first session laid this important groundwork. Next, our summit proceeded to a discussion of the role of strategic leadership in promoting scholarship and global responsibility. The papers presented in this portion of the conference demonstrate that scholarly integrity is not only a matter of the individual practices and decisions of researchers, and that strong leadership is needed at every institution to create a culture of integrity. Finally, participants highlighted and discussed the compelling issues confronting those leaders, and the institutions and countries they represented, discussing the available resources and educational activities designed to respond to those issues. In this later portion of the conference, we heard from graduate education leaders who have designed and overseen comprehensive programs as well as subject experts on particular issues.

The Florence Summit also concluded, like the Banff summit, with a discussion of future collaborative work. While the Banff summit led to nine "Banff Principles" for international collaboration in graduate education, the Florence Summit resulted in a set of consensus points that we have presented in a document entitled "Guidelines for Future Collaborations" and published in the last section of this volume. We believe the document will be equally useful to the graduate community worldwide in outlining the ethical issues involved in international collaborations.

I conclude by expressing the deepest thanks to ProQuest UMI for their generous sponsorship of this meeting and for their good partnership in making the summit possible. Their support was first and foremost financial, but equally valuable was the time they invested in discussions with participants, as active citizens in graduate global communities. The Council of Graduate Schools also gives its thanks to the virtual (and global) "program committee" who helped shape the agenda and of course to all participants for their individual and collective efforts to this volume.

Debra W. Stewart
President
Council of Graduate Schools

# II. GRADUATE EDUCATION AND SCHOLARLY INTEGRITY: MAPPING THE NATIONAL AND REGIONAL LANDSCAPE

**Summary of Presentations and Group Discussion:**

In the opening to his paper on the Australian research context, **Maxwell King** identified research ethics as an issue of increasing global importance: "Research is so important to our future lives that if we can't have confidence in the results of that research, then we're in a lot of trouble." All of the papers from the opening session of the Global Summit reflect this concern, outlining the ways in which various nations and regions are working to maintain and enhance reliable research structures. These papers also demonstrate a common concern for the status of scholarly integrity in a global context. Representing a range of regions and nations, the writers explain how their institutions are confronting issues such as the increasing mobility of scholars and the emergence of competing international standards for the responsible conduct of research.

At the same time, however, the following papers also shed light on important national and regional differences among regulatory frameworks and underscore the varying degrees of priority given to issues within the larger topic of research ethics. Representing the United States, Canada, Australia, and China respectively, **Karen Klomparens, Fred Hall, Maxwell King**, and **Shi-Gang Sun** highlight specific developments that have recently emerged in their national research landscapes: in the U.S., an active dialogue about studies using human subjects in countries that do not use the same regulations for this type of research; in Canada, an interest in strongly distinguishing the standards for ethical research in the humanities and social sciences from those in the medical sciences; in Australia, a debate about new national procedures for handling cases of research misconduct; and in China, a growing attention to the training of graduate students in all areas of research, including research integrity. Representing the European Research Council, **Pavel Exner** outlines the challenges of creating European standards for research ethics, such as benchmarks for peer review procedures. The differences in focus among these papers help demonstrate why different countries and regions may give different weight to various topics on the conference program—an important context for building toward a common set of values and plan for future work.

In the presentations and the discussion presented here, participants often use the term "culture" to refer to the common values, habits, and procedures shaping research in their various contexts. Interestingly, this term is used in a range of ways, denoting (either implicitly or explicitly) international, national *and* institutional cultures. It is helpful to underscore this flexible use of the term because it is a reminder that research cultures can be comprised of different research communities with conflicting and/or overlapping values. Research values are not determined by national culture alone, in other words, especially in the context of internationalization. For example, the papers presented here show that international networks are a growing *part* of each of the national and regional communities represented here and can support efforts to build an international academic culture of responsible and ethical research.

The discussion following the panel papers helped define two important issues that set the stage for further discussion. The first issue might best be phrased as a question: "Is it possible—and valuable— to establish a 'universal' standard for scholarly integrity and research ethics in graduate education?" **Maxwell King** provided a hypothetical example that illustrated why such a standard could be helpful, a case where a Ph.D. student in a collaborative research program between the U.S. and Australia was found guilty of research misconduct in one country, but not in the other. A number of conference participants responded to this case with concerns about the challenges of creating such a standard. Citing his own experience working with different European universities, for example, **Pavel Exner** indicated that such cases in Europe can be very difficult to resolve. Even European countries with similar cultures may disagree about how to handle violations of ethical codes, Dr. Exner added, and cited the case of two Scandinavian universities that had disagreed about the ethics violation of a student pursuing an exchange between the two institutions. Other participants questioned the practical value of a standard that seeks to include and reconcile all cultural perspectives and priorities. In particular, **Clark Hulse** raised the point that a "universal" definition of research ethics risks becoming too vague: the attempt to represent all viewpoints makes it difficult to take strong or clear positions on specific issues. This early discussion established one of the central challenges of the conference, to balance the need for specific and clear global goals for research ethics and scholarly integrity with an awareness of differences among international research communities.

The second issue emerging from the discussion concerned the best *approach* to protecting and strengthening scholarly integrity and research ethics in a global context. More specifically, participants addressed the relative value of the two most established approaches— on the one hand, demanding compliance with certain rules and procedures for ethical research, and on the other, shaping research culture through an affirmation of values such as fairness and honesty and through various forms of education. A number of participants expressed the need for universities to supplement the measures instituted by regulatory bodies with a more proactive and preventative approach. **Barbara Evans** of the University of British Columbia emphasized the need for both regulatory frameworks and education, stating that graduate leaders need to expand the emphasis on compliance to emphasize the training of future research leaders. **Mandy Thomas** of the Australian National University also pointed out the need for university leaders to address the fairness of the entire system of research, since research misconduct can grow out of a perception that rewards are unfairly distributed. These ideas, at the core of current debates about research ethics in graduate education, are discussed in greater detail in the theme-based sessions of the Global Summit.

# Scholarly Integrity in the United States: An Overview

## Karen Klomparens
## Dean of the Graduate School
## Michigan State University

### Infrastructure

The U.S. federal government has established requirements related to the responsible conduct of research (RCR) that are tied to its public research funding. These requirements are intended to foster quality research and the public's trust in that research. Each university receiving federal dollars for research must assure that it has the infrastructure to meet the federal standards governing human and animal research; chemical, radiation, and biological safety; and the handling of allegations of research misconduct. In addition, investigators funded by the two largest supporters of university research in the U.S., the National Science Foundation (NSF), which oversees research in the natural and social sciences, engineering, mathematics and related areas, and the Public Health Service (PHS,) which includes the National Institutes of Health, are required to report financial interests that might be viewed as biasing research results.

### Human Subjects Research

The U.S. was a leader in developing the Nuremberg Code following World War II. As a member of the World Medical Association, the U.S. is also committed to the 1964 Declaration of Helsinki: Ethical Principles for Medical Research involving Human Subjects.[1] The "Belmont Report" (1979) was written to establish further "Ethical Principles and Guidelines for the Protection of Human Subjects of Medical Research" specifically for U.S.-funded research.[2] The Belmont Report is, in part, the foundation upon which the U.S. developed its human subject protections via three principles: respect for individuals, beneficence (benefits of the research), and justice (fairness in costs and benefits).

Much of the U.S. focus on responsible conduct of research has been and is in the area of biomedical research and the protection of humans as research subjects. The U.S. Secretary for Health and Human Services (HHS) established the Office of Research Integrity (ORI) to promote research integrity for the U.S. Public Health Services.[3] The Office for Human Research Protections (in HHS) implements federal requirements through guidance for Institutional Review Boards that review (and approve) applications for research involving humans. The Animal Welfare Act, along with the PHS policy on humane care and use for animals in research, jointly established minimum criteria for the care and use of animals in research such as biomedical research.

## Research Misconduct

The PHS through the ORI and the NSF through its Office of the Inspector General, provide leadership in implementing the federal definition of research misconduct and the recommended processes for adjudicating allegations of research misconduct. Research misconduct is defined as falsification, fabrication, or plagiarism in proposing, performing, or reviewing research or in the reporting of research results. Procedures to investigate research misconduct must be in place in all universities that receive federal research funding. A "research integrity officer" has responsibility for carrying out required procedures, including steps such as assessment, inquiry, and/or investigation. These later steps include peers in the research discipline or related area. In the most egregious cases in which misconduct is found by an investigatory panel, a faculty investigator may find him or herself listed in the Federal Register and without the ability to receive federal funds for a number of years. A graduate student's degree may not be granted or be revoked. A program dismissal or degree revocation notation is often placed on the student's university transcript.

## General Definitions

Research integrity is commonly referred to in the natural sciences (life, biomedical, physical), engineering, and social, behavioral, and economic sciences as "responsible conduct of research." Inherent in the term is the commitment to compliance and ensuring that experiments will be set up carefully and that data will be analyzed and reported accurately, objectively, and honestly. Scholarly integrity is a broader term than RCR, as it can also encompass the scholarship created in the arts and humanities, including art, music, dance, theatre, fiction, and poetry. Research ethics usually refers to the philosophical principles that underlie the responsible conduct of research.

## Educational Programs for RCR and/or Scholarly Integrity

The ORI defines RCR to include nine areas: data acquisition, management, and control; conflict of interest and commitment; animal welfare; humans as subjects of research; research misconduct; authorship issues; peer review; mentor/mentee responsibilities and relationships; and collaborative research. Educational programs in RCR are a common strategy to educate undergraduate and graduate students about compliance with federal regulations. Each university has its own approach to content delivery and to the monitoring of compliance. For example, a student may not be able to submit a thesis in which the research used human subjects if there was no prior IRB approval. Similarly, the ability to order/purchase animals or some chemicals or radiologicals for experiments usually requires training from an explicitly defined source or set of programs. One such source is the Collaborative Institutional Training Initiative (CITI).[4] The development of CITI was partly funded by ORI. It offers online programs/modules that serve nearly 1000 institutions, including organizations in 36 countries, often in multiple languages.

## Current Initiatives

In the past few years, a focus on questionable or unacceptable actions beyond the federal definition of research misconduct has increased.[5] Other current research addresses the particularly challenging issues of conducting research using humans in international locations, often where the culture, policies, and procedures are different than one's own. The opportunities and barriers related to making progress on these new issues and the impact of these issues on the climate for scholarly integrity remains for us to collectively study and discuss.

## References

1    http://www.wma.net/e/policy/b3.htm.

2    http://ohsr.od.nih.gov/guidelines/belmont.html.

3    The homepage of the ORI can be found at http://ori.dhhs.gov/.

4    The CITI login and registration page can be accessed online at https://www.citiprogram.org/dev/default.asp?language=english.

5    Martinson BC, Anderson MS, De Vries R. (2005). Scientists Behaving Badly. *Nature*, June 9 2005; 435: 737-738.

# Graduate Education and Scholarly Integrity: The Australian Context

## Maxwell King
### Pro Vice-Chancellor, Research and Research Training
### Monash University

**How are terms such as "scholarly integrity," "research integrity," and "research ethics" defined and understood in the Australian context?**

"Scholarly integrity" is often interchangeable with "academic integrity" or "ethical scholarship" in the Australian context. The following representative definition comes from the University of Tasmania:

> "Academic integrity is about mastering the art of scholarship. Scholarship involves researching, understanding and building upon the work of others and requires that you give credit where it is due and acknowledge the contributions of others to your own intellectual efforts. At its core, academic integrity requires honesty."[1]

Notions of "research integrity" at Australian institutions are typically based around the *Australian Code for the Responsible Conduct of Research* described in the next section and on relevant national ethics legislation. "Research ethics" tends to be used more narrowly and refers to research involving animals and humans.

## What is the government agency responsible for research integrity?

There is no Office of Research Integrity in Australia. The two main government research funding organisations, the Australian Research Council (ARC) and the National Health and Medical Research Council (NHMRC) have joined with Australian universities to produce the *Australian Code for the Responsible Conduct of Research,* which was published last year. Part A of the code covers *Principles and Practices to Encourage Responsible Research Conduct* with sections on management of data, supervision of research trainees, publications and disseminations of research findings, authorship, peer review, conflicts of interest and collaborative research across institutions. Part B is entitled *Breaches of the Code, Research Misconduct, and the Framework for Resolving Allegations.* There is currently a debate about Part B of the Code due to its cross-over with other national statements and procedures (particularly in the ethics area) and where its recommendations intersect with local industrial agreements—misconduct in research is basically a primary breach of an academic's employment contract – and legislation (whistleblowers, privacy etc).

Universities and other institutions that conduct research are largely responsible for research integrity within their own institutions and will have their own codes and policies. They will need to embrace the *Australian Code* or risk losing access to research funding from the ARC and NHMRC.

## How is sanctionable misconduct defined, investigated and penalized?

For Monash University, research misconduct "means conduct in, or connection with, research that

a)   is dishonest, reckless or negligent, and
b)   seriously deviates from accepted standards within the scientific and scholarly community for proposing, conducting or reporting research."[2]

Our code then gives a range of examples.

The current procedure for investigating a complaint is as follows. The Vice-President (Research) or delegate conducts some preliminary inquiries. If he/she is satisfied that a preliminary investigation is warranted, he/she convenes a Preliminary Investigation Committee to determine whether a case exists that research misconduct has occurred. The President then considers the report of the committee and decides what action to take. This may include disciplinary procedures, or further investigation on the establishment of a formal committee of enquiry. Serious misconduct can lead to a range of penalties including termination of employment.

## What are the implications for graduate-level educational practice?

An allegation of research misconduct by a student would be investigated by a preliminary review panel. If that panel determines a prima facie case of research misconduct, then a Research Graduate Discipline Committee is formed to hear and determine the matter (including penalties).

I believe at most universities, research ethics (as narrowly defined) is covered well. A recent survey conducted on graduates from the eight research intensive universities (Group of Eight) five years from graduation, suggested that research ethics had received an even greater emphasis than necessary. An area where I believe we need improvement is research integrity (teaching students to give sufficient credit to others' work and avoiding plagiarism). This is a topic we have left to supervisors (mentors), although this may be slowly changing, with some universities running seminars for their students on this topic.

## References

1    http://www.academicintegrity.utas.edu.au/.

2    http://mrgs.monash.edu.au/research/doctoral/archive/handbook_cd_2007/handbook/chapter8b.html.

# Canadian Policies and Practices Regarding Ethical Conduct of Research

## Fred L. Hall
### Vice-Provost of Graduate Education
### University of Calgary

With regard to research ethics policies (to paraphrase Charles Dickens), Canada has the best of situations; Canada has the worst of situations. For a decade now, the three federal granting councils have coordinated their policies with regard to research ethics, so there is no conflict among the granting agencies in their ethics requirements. However, the social scientists and humanists have been of the view that this coordination has forced them into a medical approvals type of process that is excessive given the limited potential hazards from their research. In response to these concerns, the Interagency Advisory Panel on Research Ethics (PRE) created a Social Sciences and Humanities Research Ethics Special Working Committee in November 2002, which has been active in producing a number of reports[1] dealing with issues in those disciplines.

The PRE itself was created in November 2001, and was "mandated by the Canadian Institutes of Health Research (CIHR), the Natural Sciences and Engineering Research Council (NSERC), and the Social Sciences and Humanities Research Council (SSHRC), to promote high ethical standards of conduct in research involving humans through the development, evolution, interpretation, and implementation of the *Tri-Council Policy Statement: Ethical Conduct for Research Involving Humans* (TCPS). The Agencies adopted the TCPS, in August 1998, as a common research ethics policy for those conducting, participating in, or reviewing human research in institutions funded by CIHR, NSERC and SSHRC."[2] "Additionally, several Canadian federal government organizations, such as the National Research Council, the Canadian Space Agency, Health Canada and National Defence, have adopted the TCPS. Some professional bodies and provincial government departments use it as well."[3]

These three agencies provide the bulk of the federal funding for university research, and also have major programs of direct scholarship support to graduate students. Compliance with the Tri-Council Policy Statement[4] is important for every university in the country, and hence for each faculty and graduate student researcher. In accordance with the TCPS, each institution has established one or more research Ethics Boards (REB) which is responsible for reviewing proposals. REB approval is needed before research can begin: "The REB ... has both educational and review roles. The REB serves the research community as a consultative body and thus contributes to education in research ethics; it also has responsibility for independent, multidisciplinary review of the ethics of research to determine whether the research should be permitted to start or to continue."[5]

Interestingly, none of the three terms asked about in the instructions for this paper, "scholarly integrity," "research integrity," and/or "research ethics," are explicitly defined in the TCPS. A probable reason for this absence is that the primary focus of the policy is on those who bear the risks of the research[6] rather than on the scholars or researchers.

The frameworks for addressing allegations of research misconduct are not contained within the TCPS. Indeed, an electronic search of the Policy for 'misconduct' does not find any use of the word. One has to turn to the individual granting councils to find any discussion of a policy framework for addressing misconduct. The NSERC site says that each institution must have "appropriate impartial and accountable procedures" to receive allegations of misconduct in research and scholarship; conduct appropriate enquiries; protect the privacy of the accused and of the accuser as far as is possible; allow the accused due process and full opportunity to respond to the allegations; decide whether or not there has been misconduct; and determine the actions to be taken as a result.[7] The SSHRC site has identical wording; the CIHR site refers one to the NSERC site.

The procedures for handling allegations of academic misconduct are frequently different for faculty than for graduate students, which can create problems. Also, although REB's operate on each campus and consist largely of members of the campus communities, they are accountable to the federal granting councils, not to the institutions in which they function. The councils require each institution to have mechanisms to address misconduct, but the institution cannot require the REB to play any role in those mechanisms, because it is answerable to the councils, not to the university.[8]

Where misconduct is found to have occurred, the institution is free to set its own penalty. As with the procedures, the penalties or sanctions for graduate students tend to differ considerably from those for faculty members. The relevant granting council may also choose to impose a sanction. The sanctions identified on the NSERC site include refusing to consider future funding applications, refusing to pay future grant installments, and requesting refund of money already paid to the researcher. In addition, the NSERC stipulates, "As agencies of the federal government, the Councils retain the right at any time to bring a case to the attention of the appropriate legal authorities."[9]

CGS asks, "What are the implications of these policy frameworks for graduate-level educational practice?" Although the TCPS and PRE have educational mandates, little appears to have been done at that level to date. An on-line tutorial was created in 2004, but it is a tutorial on the TCPS itself, not on research ethics or integrity more broadly. An educational subcommittee of the PRE was established, but their only report to date has been on educating the community members of the REB, not on educating researchers. So, to be blunt, the implications of this policy framework for graduate level education has been simply to educate students in the steps needed to work through the REB process rather than to open any broader discussion of scholarly integrity.

# References

1    http://www.pre.ethics.gc.ca/english/workgroups/sshwc.cfm, 28 July 2008.

2    http://www.pre.ethics.gc.ca/english/aboutus/mandate.cfm, 28 July 2008.

3    http://www.pre.ethics.gc.ca/english/faq/frequentlyaskedquestions.cfm, Question #6, 28 July 2008.

4    Canadian Institutes of Health Research, Natural Sciences and Engineering Research Council of Canada, Social Sciences and Humanities Research Council of Canada, *Tri-Council Policy Statement: Ethical Conduct for Research Involving Humans.* 1998 (with 2000, 2002 and 2005 amendments). The official version is the on-line version, the English version of which is found (28 July 2008) at http://www.pre.ethics.gc.ca/english/policystatement/policystatement.cfm.

5    http://www.pre.ethics.gc.ca/english/policystatement/section1.cfm#1B, 28 July 2008.

6    http://www.pre.ethics.gc.ca/english/policystatement/goals.cfm#B, endnote 3, 28 July 2008.

7    http://www.nserc.gc.ca/professors_e.asp?nav=profnav&lbi=p9, section 2b, 28 July 2008.

8    Thanks to Susan Pfeiffer for reminding me of this point.

9    http://www.nserc.gc.ca/professors_e.asp?nav=profnav&lbi=p9    final sentence, 28 July 2008.

# Graduate Education in China: The New Horizon and Perspectives

## Shi-Gang Sun
### On behalf of Association of Chinese Graduate Schools (ACGS)
### Vice-President and Dean of the Graduate School
### Xiamen University

The history of cultivating master's and doctoral degree graduates in China can be dated back to the early decades of the 20th century. The earliest document about master's or doctoral degree conferment was written in 1908.

Modern graduate education was reinvigorated starting in 1978. The total number of graduate students during the first 20 years, from 1978 to 1998, amounted to about 700,000, among whom less than 100,000 were Ph.D candidates. In the last 10 years, graduate education has been boosted. The quantity of graduate students on the campus of Chinese universities has today reached about 1.2 million, which is slightly less than the number for the United States, placing China in the 2nd place in the world for the number of graduate students. The fast development of graduate education in China during the last decade has been pushed, on the one hand, by the fast development of the economy, and on the other hand, by the Chinese government's strategy of building world-ranking universities in China. The "211" and "985" projects are the two important schemes of the strategy. The "211" project involves one hundred universities in which the Chinese government invests a significant amount of money to enhance the competence of key disciplines. For the "985" project, the Chinese government selected only 39 top-ranking Chinese universities and allocated to each university at least a few hundred million Chinese Yuan to improve research facilities and to recruit high-quality faculty members.

Since the very beginning of the development of graduate education in 1978, quality assurance has always been the core issue. This has been accomplished in the following phases.

(1)     Infrastructure. There are now over 2,000 Universities in China; only 484 Universities can confer Master's degrees, and 259 Universities can award doctoral degrees. However, the major activities of graduate education were carried out in 56 key universities, all of which have graduate schools. It is worth mentioning that all 56

universities were involved in the "211" and "985" projects, i.e. they have obtained strong support from the Chinese government, and have excellent research facilities and high-quality professorship teams.

(2) Integrity in research. In 2007, the Education Ministry of China announced the innovative plan to promote graduate education through national learning forums for graduates, summer schools, academic conferences, and through mutual visits and exchanges of graduate students between universities and the institutes of the Chinese Academy of Sciences.

(3) Graduate study-abroad programs. Under the support of the Chinese Scholarship Council, there are about 6,000 scholarships that can be distributed to graduate students for study abroad, either to do research in a foreign institute or university laboratory under the framework of the "co-tutelle," or to obtain a foreign Ph.D. degree.

(4) Reform of graduate education. In the last two years, some Chinese universities have started trying to reform graduate education. The key points of this reform aim to enhance the competence of graduate students, to promote research conditions for graduate students, and to enhance the responsibility of professors who serve as supervisors or advisors to graduate students. This year the reform will be carried out in all universities that have set up graduate schools.

(5) The Associations of Chinese Graduate Schools (ACGS). The ACGS was founded in November 1999 and approved by the Education Ministry of China. The membership of ACGS is limited to the deans or the executive deans of the 23 graduate schools formally registered and the 23 graduate schools provisionally registered at the Education Ministry. The objectives of ACGS are to promote the construction and administration of graduate schools, especially for the purpose of enhancing the quality of graduate students; to foster the common interests of graduate school deans; to advise the policy and strategy of graduate education in China; and to exchange information with foreign associations of graduate education.

# Graduate Education and Research Ethics from the Viewpoint of the European Research Council

## Pavel Exner
### ERC Scientific Council Member

### What is the European Research Council (ERC)?

The name belongs to an all-European funding organization created by the decision of the European Commission and Parliament in the beginning of 2007; these institution pledged to guarantee its autonomy and independence. The ERC is thus rather young and in the process of a fast development; at the present time it is finishing its second round of grant calls. Since the main goal of the ERC is to support *excellent research of a frontier type,* it can only influence graduate education processes in an indirect way. Nevertheless, many ERC grants involve the participation of graduate student researchers, who must follow the ethical standards set for ERC projects.

### How is the ERC organized?

The ERC strategic and tactical aims are decided by the Scientific Council (ScC), which is composed of 22 renowned European scientists. They represent neither their countries nor any other entity—only their personal scientific experience. The ScC is complemented by a "dedicated implementation structure" currently under transformation into a full-fledged executive agency and charged with the realization of the ScC decisions. The peer review process of grant applications is controlled by topical panels formed by the ScC from experienced scientists.

### What grants does the ERC award?

As mentioned above, the ERC's goal is to support excellent research with a preference for "frontier" projects that cross traditional research area boundaries. There are two main types of grants, Starting Grants aiming at young researchers and Advanced Grants without any age limits. In both cases the only selection criterion is the *excellence of the project.* Nobody is excluded on national grounds, within Europe as well as outside, and no other eligibility restrictions are imposed; the only requirement is that (a dominant part of) the research is performed in Europe.

## Standardizing Grant Policy

One of the aims of the ERC, in general terms, is to set benchmarks for European research, which is notoriously plagued by a wide variety of practices for distributing research support as well as different peer review standards. This variety also applies to *research ethics,* an idea which is often interpreted differently in different national contexts. The aim of the ERC is to promote *best practices* in all our granting processes.

## Conflict of Interest

The ERC is a young organization that is in the process of implementing its various functions. One of the first things we did was to formulate rules concerning conflict of interest in the peer review process. We started from the *strictest version* ruling, e.g., that belonging to the same organization as the principal investigator excludes a person from refereeing, and only later we will seek a common-sense balance (recall that in countries like France, where the CNRS is interrelated with most universities, this policy would practically exclude the whole country).

## Other Ethical Issues

The diversity of the European research landscape can introduce other dangers, such as parallel funding of the same project from national and European resources. To counter this problem we have included a strict *funding identifier* into our grant applications. At the same time, we worked out *redress procedures* not only to address formal errors but also to give the applicants the right to complain when they think they were harmed by the panels or the referees.

## Early Results

The results of the first year and a half of ERC activity inspire some optimism. The Scientific Council is regularly monitoring all the procedures and its members were happy to see that the mechanisms we have managed to devise so far worked well. It is the beginning of a long process, of course, and many challenges lie ahead. This brief survey could only sketch what the European Research Council is doing and I will be happy to answer your questions.

# III. COMPARING INSTITUTIONAL APPROACHES: CREATING A CULTURE SUPPORTIVE OF RESEARCH AND SCHOLARLY INTEGRITY

## Summary of Presentations and Group Discussion

The third session of the 2008 Global Summit was designed to compare institutional approaches to fostering a culture of research integrity in relation to four key questions:

- What is the role of the university and university leadership, specifically, in advancing research integrity at your institution?
- What are the barriers and opportunities in your institutional context for enhanced approaches to research ethics and scholarly integrity?
- How are graduate experiences and/or the institutional environment assessed?
- What specific issues do you face in educating a multinational community for careers in research?

While these questions proved to be interrelated, they also raised more specific problems and issues that university leaders often confront in their efforts to support an ethical research culture.

For the segment on the role of university leadership, participants focused on a number of different communication structures within the university. **Lisa Tedesco** of Emory University explained that her institution's strategic plan and vision statement place emphasis on the aims and values of its research community. Dr. Tedesco indicated that these statements go beyond the enforcement of policies and procedures: they remind both researchers and administrators that the university defines itself according to core values, aiming to use research to support the public good. In his presentation on Nanjing University, **Chong-Qing Cheng** explained how university leaders can emphasize broad institutional values in their communications with faculty. Because young faculty face great pressure to publish, Dr. Cheng stated, it is important for university leaders to stress the importance of quality over quantity in publication. Finally, **Richard Russell**'s paper focused on specific programs supporting research integrity at the University of Adelaide. Because these programs are diverse, supporting the needs of different groups of researchers, leaders must organize cooperative efforts between various stakeholders at the institution, ensuring the support and understanding of all groups.

Addressing barriers and opportunities to institutional change, participants discussed institutional efforts to create a higher level of investment in, and engagement with, ethical questions related to research among graduate students. **Karen Klomparens** of Michigan State University gave special attention to the issue of graduate student motivation. While graduate students must comply with ethical codes in order to secure research funding, she noted, they often lack the motivation to pursue additional opportunities in ethics education. To meet this challenge, Michigan State communicates to students that training in research ethics offers long-term professional advantages, not just the immediate reward of funding. **Susan Pfeiffer** of the University of Toronto also outlined some of the challenges faced by her university in responding to graduate students who place low value on RCR training. Dr. Pfeiffer noted that providing students with resources in the responsible conduct of research within their individual graduate programs has been the most effective strategy of ethics training, but she also outlined some broader institutional tools. For example, at her university, graduate students in the medical sciences can elect to take an oath of professionalism and ethical conduct.

The third topic, assessment, focused on measuring the relationship between official university statements of values and institutional practice. One method of assessing the distance between policy and practice was suggested by **Suzanne Ortega** of the University of Mexico, who proposed that graduate schools conduct an "inventory" of the rewards and resources allocated to university faculty to ensure that behaviors promoting the responsible conduct of research were recognized and rewarded. Dr. Ortega also noted that new tools have recently been developed to measure the transparency and fairness of ethical rules within university communities and to understand whether official rules are consistently enforced. Such tools were generally viewed as an important new resource for gaining a more comprehensive understanding of university research environments.

In the final panel, participants addressed the challenges of presenting ethics education to a multinational group of graduate students. **Christine Keitel-Kreidt** of the Freie University Berlin reintroduced an issue raised earlier—the value of affirming the connection between research and the public good. Describing the efforts of her university to encourage the Turkish immigrant population in Germany to pursue careers in research, Dr. Keitel-Kreidt emphasized that equal opportunity for researchers demonstrates a commitment to ensuring that research is not dominated by the interests of society's most powerful or elite members. **Fred Hall** of the University of Calgary examined the complexities of ethics education when the backgrounds of the students vary considerably. Dr. Hall's presentation raised questions about the common institutional strategy of providing identical ethics training for all students, and raised the possibility that it might be more effective to provide international students with a specialized ethics training course. Part of his paper outlined the advantages and disadvantages of a separate ethics training course for non-Canadian graduate students.

The problem of providing specialized ethics training to non-native students received significant attention in the discussion following the presentations. One of the subtopics that emerged within this discussion was the link between weak language skills and ethics violations. More specifically, participants discussed the perception that students who have difficulty communicating in the language they use for scholarship are more tempted to plagiarize or break ethical codes. Representing a university where English is the dominant language, **Dr. Russell** suggested that universities need to address this problem before students matriculate; transcripts and scores on English proficiency exams are not necessarily strong indicators, he stated, of a student's ability to communicate effectively in English within his or her academic discipline. **Dr. Pfeiffer** and **Dr. Hulse** approached this issue from a different perspective, questioning the perception that international students are indeed the most likely to violate ethics codes. In response to Dr. Hall's presentation, for example, Dr. Pfeiffer indicated that while the greater proportion of ethics violations are made by international students, some of the most serious violations are made by native students. This discussion suggested that leaders in graduate education are seeking more information about the reasons behind a higher numbers of reported cases of research misconduct cases among international students—crucial information for effectively addressing this challenge.

Research ethics training raised additional issues for universities working to build their status in the global community. **Isaac Mazonde** of the University of Botswana stated that his university is working to create structures for helping students and staff to become more sensitive to the research ethics standards that are more prevalent outside Botswana's borders; many students arrive at the university without any exposure to research ethics training. Dr. Mazonde's remarks underlined the fact that university leaders can most effectively cultivate a common culture of responsible research if they are familiar with the range of cultural backgrounds represented by graduate students and faculty.

Participants in this final session also discussed strategies for increasing students' level of commitment to, and reflective engagement with, institutional ethical guidelines. Many participants spoke about the importance of demonstrating that all members of the community—administration, faculty, and students—are accountable to the ethical codes of the university. Several ideas for formalizing this multi-level commitment were put forward. **Barbara Evans** remarked, for example, that if graduate students are required to take an oath to conduct their work with scholarly integrity, then perhaps faculty should be required to take an oath affirming their ethical responsibilities to students. **Karen DePauw** also noted that her university, like others in Virginia, subscribes to a Graduate Honor System that requires students to provide a signed promise that they will abide by the honor system. Throughout the presentations and discussions, it was agreed that it is important for universities to demonstrate that university leaders stand behind, and apply to all those involved in the research enterprise, the ethical codes outlined in regulatory frameworks.

# The Role of the University and University Leadership in Advancing Research Integrity

## Lisa A. Tedesco
### Vice Provost, Academic Affairs and Dean of the Graduate School
### Emory University

This very brief essay is designed to answer the question, *"What is the role of the university and university leadership, specifically, in advancing research integrity at your institution?"* Let me begin by providing some basic characteristics of Emory University and describing our mission, development, and the projected course of recent strategic planning.

Emory University is a leading international research university, in Atlanta, Georgia, the largest international metropolitan center in the southeast region of the United States. We are also home to Emory Healthcare, one of the southeast region's largest and most comprehensive healthcare systems. The University is comprised of a liberal arts college, five professional schools (medicine, law, nursing, public health and theology) and a graduate school that awards the PhD and master's degrees in over 40 program areas. Our campus is contiguous with the Centers for Disease Control and Prevention and we have collaborative relationships with CARE USA and the Carter Center. Emory has over 3600 faculty, 12,570 students from 50 states and 117 countries and over 24,400 employees. In 2007, Emory investigators received $383.9M in sponsored research funding. Our size, and the concentrated geography of our campus, allows us to boast of an "authentic interdisciplinarity" where scholars from all areas can easily and readily interact in research, scholarly, and creative collaborations.

As is the case with all major research universities in the United States, there are clear and present guidelines for the responsible conduct of scholarship and research and they can usually be found in standardized policy formats on the websites of vice-presidents for research. At Emory, our guidelines are based on three important principles. They are:

1. "the University is obligated to protect and foster academic freedom and intellectual integrity for all members of the University community;

2. "the University is accountable to outside funding sources that support the scholarship and research of its faculty; and

3. "every scholar has ultimate responsibility for the accuracy and validity of his/her own work and that of junior co-investigators with whom she/he establishes collaborative relationships."[1]

These principles at Emory (and their parallels at sister institutions in the US) map to a series of guidelines and practices for compliance that are applicable to scholarship and research in the humanities, social sciences, and natural and biomedical sciences.

University presidents and other leaders and officers are held accountable by their boards of trustees and regents to "hold the University in trust for the future." At its core, this accountability on the part of university leadership must ensure these practices and by implication a promise of institutional (organizational *and* individual) habits and a positive climate created by attitudes, values, beliefs and intentions to hold the University in trust for the future in service to the public good. More specifically, Emory's leadership, from faculty leaders, to the President and Provost up to the Board of Trustees, has shaped a very compelling vision for the University. Our vision statement states that Emory University

"is an inquiry-driven, ethically engaged, and diverse community whose members work collaboratively for positive transformation in the world through courageous leadership in teaching, research, scholarship, health care, and social action."[2]

Further extending this vision statement is a university-wide strategic plan that is ambitiously titled, *"Where Courageous Inquiry Leads."* When one reads the plan, it is clear that the University is committing an array of resources to be a leader, locally, nationally, and internationally in addressing, as our literature states,

"some of the world's toughest challenges and greatest opportunities—from religion, conflict, and peace building, to race and social difference, to issues of global health and new understandings of what makes us human. Implementation of Emory's strategic plan will transform its campus and positively influence local and global communities."

With this vision statement and the strategic directions that commit the University to grow and develop along certain dimensions – through work that defines aspirations in global and complex terms – a renewal through *recommitment* is placed on the value, meaning and action for research and scholarly integrity. The work is not only about holding the University in trust for the future, but also about *reaching our aspirations* through ethically engaged courageous inquiry, by serving the public good. What new pressures does this place on the call for integrity?

At Emory, our leaders must insure the fundamental resources to develop a culture that persists in values and behaviors for research integrity at all levels. Research directors, project managers, department chairs, and mentors must persist in their implementation and evaluation of programs and policies, and infrastructure to support research and scholarly integrity.

Because the questions we are asking and the problems we are seeking to solve are increasingly complex, the research methods and approaches to scholarly inquiry are increasingly interdisciplinary. Academic leaders must work to find resources that support complex inquiry including investigations of the nuances of integrity issues. There will be continuing need for training and education, and at Emory a growing reliance on programs from our Ethics Center.[3]

One final observation I'd like to emphasize, one that we all know well, is that research is the fulcrum of the academic community. This notion is so commonly accepted that it is used as an example for the word 'fulcrum' in English dictionaries. Graduate education and the graduate school is the mighty lever that sits on that fulcrum. As academic leaders, we must seize the opportunity to use it in powerful ways to advance research and scholarly integrity.

## References

1    Emory University, Policy 7.9, Guidelines for Responsible Conduct of Scholarship and Research, April 30, 2007, http://policies.emory.edu/7.9.

2    See Vision Statement at http://www.emory.edu/home/about/administration/president/vision.html.

3    Emory Center for Ethics, http://www.ethics.emory.edu/.

# What is the Role of the University and University Leadership in Advancing Research Integrity at the University of Adelaide?

**Richard A. Russell AM PhD DSc**
**Pro Vice-Chancellor (Research Operations)**
**and Dean of Graduate Studies**
**University of Adelaide**

Although Australian Universities are self-regulating, autonomous bodies, they are nevertheless required to conform to a number of codes and protocols, which include a wide range of ethical issues relating to research practice. The key documents include:

## General Research Ethics
*Australian Code for the Responsible Conduct of Research*
http://www.nhmrc.gov.au/index.htm

## Human Ethics
*National Statement on Ethical Conduct in Human Research (2007)*
http://www.nhmrc.gov.au/publications/synopses/e72syn.htm

## Animal Ethics
*Australian code of practice for the care and use of animals for scientific purposes, 7ᵗʰ Edition (2004)*
http://www.nhmrc.gov.au/publications/synopses/ea16syn.htm

*Animal Welfare SA Department for Environment and Heritage*
http://www.environment.sa.gov.au/animalwelfare/

*Genetically Modified Organisms*
http://www.adelaide.edu.au/ethics/genetech/

*Quarantine Act 1908*
http://www.comlaw.gov.au/ComLaw/Legislation/ActCompilation1.nsf/0/8B2
E82DCE715E4F5CA256F71004E7CF5/$file/Quarantine1908.pdf

## Responsibility

At the University of Adelaide and most other Australian Universities, the responsibility for compliance with these codes lies in the Office of the Deputy Vice-Chancellor and Vice-President (Research). Indeed, most codes contain a statement that requires oversight to be provided by a senior leader within the institution, and in some instances, vest disciplinary action with the Vice-Chancellor and President. In practical terms, at Adelaide, these codes are administered through the PVC (Research Operations) who is also responsible for the Research Ethics Compliance Unit (http://www.adelaide.edu.au/ethics/) and the Adelaide Graduate Centre.

Whilst these various codes help draw a boundary around ethics, they are not necessarily simple to operate when breeches occur, as each area has its own specific requirements and there is little uniformity of process, i.e. Animal Ethics is actually handled by a committee constituted by and reporting to the State Minister rather than to the University. Nevertheless, there are clearly defined pathways and processes for managing the small number of cases that arise.

## Education

Education on Research Ethics and Integrity is multifaceted. All new students are given a brief overview of ethical issues and who is responsible for them at their Graduate School induction. Attendance at this event is compulsory and all students are given a handbook which leads them to the various sites they may need.[1] Before students are formally confirmed in their candidature they must provide documentation of the various ethical approvals need for their work.

Different training programs have been developed for specific kinds of research. The Research Ethics Compliance Unit provides day-long introductory workshops on Animal Ethics and these are supported, where necessary, with specific courses run by the University Animal Welfare Officer. Genetically Modified Organisms and Quarantine courses are provided face-to-face at least once a year for all new users and, where necessary, staff and students are certified to operate at different containment levels. Human Ethics is now addressed by a consortium program spread across a number of Tertiary Institutions. Training programs are open to staff and students who work in relevant areas.

In terms of General Research Ethics and Scholarly Integrity, the Adelaide

Graduate Centre runs a special program for our overseas HDR (research higher degree) students called the Integrated Bridging Program. This deals at some length with the issue of plagiarism, as well as the broader aspects of adapting to the expectations of Australian university education. This is supported by online self-help modules available to all staff and students. There is also a special series of training modules entitled "Future Research Leaders" for Early Career Researchers.[2] This series of short courses provides a half-day module discussing scholarly integrity and research ethics.

As issues of misconduct fall within the scope of employment conditions, adapting to new codes is an interesting exercise that involves quite a number of people. The Research Intensive Universities in Australia (the Go8) are currently working through this process and, when it is complete, Adelaide will move to introduce an online and certifiable course for all new staff.

## Barriers and Opportunities

There are no barriers to enhancing these areas as they are seen as an integral part of University research culture. There is a high level of cooperation between the divisions of Human Resources, Prudential Services and the Office of the DVC and VP(R). This cooperation not only insures that Ethics and Integrity have the full support of senior management within the University, but that reviews and planning involve all the key stakeholders in the institution.

Nevertheless, most academics (students and staff), find reading policy a low priority task and there is a need to regularly review educational support, particularly in the light of any breeches that may occur, especially those which appear to arise from the "publish or perish" syndrome.

## Evaluation of Student Experiences

At the time they submit their theses, all students are required to complete a confidential online survey recording their experiences. Whilst students reserve the right to submit a blank form, most choose to answer all, or at least the majority of, questions as well as provide free text commentary. These surveys are reviewed annually and inform the General Quality Cycle employed by the Adelaide Graduate Centre. Ethical issues do not appear to be a major issue for students and are hence difficult to summarise. Plagiarism, Authorship and IP are the three issues which do elicit comment, and indeed these issues are the major challenges in multicultural institutions.

There is also a National Survey conducted externally, but it is our experience that we get more useful feedback from our local survey because questions are raised at a time when experiences are fresh in the student's mind.

## Notes and References

1    www.adelaide.edu.au/graduatecentre/handbook.

2    These were developed and evaluated by the Go8 Universities.

# Opportunities and Barriers
# for Enhanced Approaches to Scholarly Integrity

## Karen L. Klomparens
## Dean of the Graduate School
## Michigan State University

The U.S. government requires "assurances" from each institution receiving federal funds that effective infrastructure is in place to meet federal guidelines on human and animals in research; chemical, radiation, and biological safety; and the handling of allegations of misconduct in research. In addition, a process to manage potential financial conflicts of interest is required. The two most common funding agencies for U.S. research, the National Institutes of Health and the National Science Foundation (NSF), require educational programs for the responsible conduct of research (RCR) for graduate students on training grants, and more recently, for graduate students and postdoctoral trainees on any/all NSF-funded research projects.

As mandates connected to funding, these requirements remove the barrier of inertia, and in part, assure a starting point for a minimum level of RCR compliance and scholarly integrity. On the MSU campus, as on many others, there is an interconnected set of policies and practices across multiple offices that focuses on compliance. Many U.S. graduate deans place a priority on opportunities to provide and/or encourage RCR programs that go beyond compliance to include broader educational goals focused on scholarly integrity and on the development of an educational climate with a minimum of "questionable" research practices.

For example, at Michigan State University, education and training is mandatory for all personnel (faculty, graduate students, technicians, postdoctoral trainees, undergraduates) who work with human or animal subjects and for chemical, radiation, and biological safety. MSU requires completion of online educational modules, which must be periodically updated, in order to submit proposals to the institutional review board (IRB) related to Human Subjects and for Animal Care and Use or to purchase animals and/or laboratory chemicals. No theses or dissertations using human subjects are accepted without assurance of this training and prior IRB approval. MSU participates in the Collaborative Institutional Training Initiative (CITI) as part of our required training.[1]

Workshops in RCR were begun by the Graduate School, in cooperation with the Office of the Vice President for Research and Graduate Studies, in late 1998. The workshops were refined and integrated into a series in 2000 that stressed "responsibility" as a unifying educational approach.[2] These workshops are part of an overall effort in the Graduate School to emphasize the career and professional development of graduate students. The workshop series goal was not simply to enforce compliance with regulatory requirements, but rather to stimulate discussion and to complement discipline-specific RCR training in the graduate programs. In this case, the RCR program focuses on scholarly integrity as an explicit and essential component of graduate student professional development. Workshops are offered in the early evenings, with a light meal, in order to avoid the common stated barrier of "not enough time" to participate.

Often, a crisis is the best opportunity to inspire or provoke change or to decrease the significance of a stated (real or not) barrier. In the past decade, research misconduct investigations involving graduate students on our own campus, as well as public visibility of high-profile cases of alleged misconduct elsewhere, served to stimulate initiatives to focus faculty and graduate students on the need to advance our collective efforts on enhancing the climate for scholarly integrity.

For example, in 2003, a University Task Force on Research Mentoring of Graduate Students established a foundation for institutionalizing RCR education by developing *Guidelines for Graduate Student Advising and Mentoring Relationships* and *Guidelines for Integrity in Research and Creative Activities.*[3] Chaired by a member of the National Academy of Sciences, Hans Kende, the task force of faculty and graduate students represented the five largest colleges at MSU. The University Graduate Council (our elected and representative faculty governance body that includes graduate students) endorsed the report in February 2004 and approved an additional four recommendations. The University's Faculty and Academic Councils approved all recommendations.

The Task Force recommended that the two sets of guidelines be explicitly included in all graduate handbooks of departments, schools, and interdisciplinary units. The Graduate School implemented these recommendations and reviewed all handbooks for "completeness" in 2005.[4] With the visibility and implementation of the Mentoring Task Force recommendations, plus federally-mandated RCR compliance connected to funding, selected graduate programs in the basic biomedical sciences began requiring their newly admitted students to attend the RCR workshops provided by the Graduate School.

In 2007, two new collaborative initiatives (Graduate School, VP for Research and Graduate Studies, and Provost/VP for Academics) began in order to expand our efforts to highlight the importance of scholarly integrity and responsible research practices. The Hans Kende Memorial Lecture Series on Integrity and Mentoring in Research sponsored public (and provocative) presentations by nationally recognized experts. In addition, a Research Integrity Council was appointed by the Provost and VP for Research and Graduate Studies to "assess our status and continue our collective commitment to fostering an environment where responsible conduct in research is valued and protected."

As these efforts enter their second year, we intend to leverage the opportunity provided by the new NSF mandate for RCR education and to continue efforts to promote scholarly integrity across the campus through initiatives of our Research Integrity Council. In addition, we intend to focus on the broader questions of the climate for scholarly integrity by integrating current research by Brian Martinson et. al.[5] on the unacceptable or questionable research practices that fall outside the U.S. federal definition of misconduct, but nonetheless, can have a negative impact on graduate education and graduate students.

## Notes and References

1    See https://www.citiprogram.org/citidocuments/aboutus.htm.

2    See http://grad.msu.edu/all/respconduct.htm.

3    http://grad.msu.edu/all/ris04.pdf.

4    The handbook template and approved versions of graduate handbooks are available online at http://grad.msu.edu/staff/ght.htm.

5    Martinson BC, Anderson MS, De Vries R. (2005). Scientists Behaving Badly. *Nature*, June 9 2005; 435: 737-738.

# Research Ethics and Scholarly Integrity: Institutional Initiatives and Barriers to Effective Interventions

Susan Pfeiffer
Dean of Graduate Studies and Vice-Provost, Graduate Education
University of Toronto

As reported in a recent survey undertaken at Dalhousie University (Nova Scotia), graduate students know that training in research ethics is available, but they place a low value on it. When asked to rank the priority of a workshop on "ethical considerations in the academic workplace," faculty members ranked this topic at 19 (with 1 being highest), and graduate students ranked it at 34.[1] In Canada (see Fred Hall's commentary), the oversight of research ethics and integrity is handled federally and there is a focus on the enforcement of standards in research involving human subjects. The federal agencies (Tri-Council) provide an online training module that introduces the guidelines and the approval mechanisms. Canadian universities provide training to graduate students who must get Research Ethics Board (REB) permission to undertake research. While there is no standardization of universities' training modules, their common goal likely will be to convey a skill set (getting approval). They may or may not emphasize the development of a mind-set (responsible conduct of research). The investigation of alleged misconduct is handled by each institution, following protocols that have been vetted by the federal agencies. The confidentiality associated with these investigations precludes their use as cautionary tales, and hinders our abilities to develop pan-institutional dialogue.

Responsibility for the development of professional skills in research ethics and integrity falls to institutions under each province's degree level expectations. Those who complete a graduate degree in Ontario are expected to possess the skills necessary for "ethical behavior consistent with academic integrity and the use of appropriate guidelines and procedures for responsible conduct of research."[2] Thus, federal agencies deal with enforcement and provincial agencies deal with education/training. In recent months, this federal-provincial conflict played itself out in predictable form when the federal Tri-Council drafted a set of expectations about professional skills development, then ceased further development of the initiative, in response to concerns that arose during consultations, including the sense that the Tri-Council initiative was in conflict with provincial responsibilities and institutional autonomy. At the University of Toronto, with over 13,000 graduate students enrolled in over 150 programs that are delivered on multiple sites, we normally find that initiatives at the level of the graduate program are most effective. There are some institutional tools, however. In addition to briefings on the REB, the University of Toronto Office of the Vice-President Research offers workshops within a broader series called Graduate Student Initiatives (GSI). Some are oriented toward ethics in the social sciences and humanities, and others focus on the link between entrepreneurship and integrity. The MaRS Discovery District provides a very popular Entrepreneurship 101 Lecture Series.[3] Several graduate programs in the life sciences urge or require their students to complete the online course, Protecting Human Research Participants, developed and supported by the NIH Office of Extramural Research. Since completion of this tutorial is a requirement for all researchers receiving NIH funding, it is seen as a valuable exercise. In the Faculty of Applied Science and Engineering, required seminars and a web page address the topic of ethics in graduate research, tailored to that context. Our Education faculty has adopted a similar approach.[4]

In 2007, the Institute of Medical Science developed a new *graduate student oath.* This unit hosts a large number of researching graduate students, with about 200 MSc and 200 PhD students. As described in the journal *Science* (320:1587-1588, 2008), the oath "focuses on three elements of scientific training at the graduate level: community, professionalism and ethical conduct." It is voluntarily recited at the first meeting of the new graduate class each autumn, and each person then receives a printed copy of the text. The Oath Booklet contains references to the relevant policies, and commentary that supports the importance of integrity in scientific research. The institute's requirements subsequently reinforce the concepts introduced in the oath. Advocates of the oath suggest that it should be a standard requirement of graduate study in the life sciences, and should provide the cornerstone for modules addressing community, professionalism and ethical conduct. A national newspaper covered the development as "Scientists get their own Hippocratic Oath."[5] While this approach was being developed for research-oriented students, the University was also establishing a broad new Policy on Standards for Professional Practice Behavior for Health Profession Students. This encompasses not only medical fields but also social work, pharmacy, clinical psychology, physical education and others. It replaces a number of older discipline-based policies.

Challenges for the future include the following: While we have mechanisms to enforce good behavior and penalize bad behavior, we have few structures that encourage intellectual engagement that considers the principles that underlie research integrity. Mechanisms are established that strongly encourage ethical behavior in research, especially in the life sciences. In some sectors of the life sciences, a strong educational framework is developing. We have made modest progress in translating the achievements of our colleagues in the life sciences into other academic domains. There is a clear need for leadership and vision in the area of education for research integrity, so that all graduate students understand the reasoning behind the behavioral expectations and how those expectations apply to their research areas. In sum, our fundamental barrier is the absence of federal-provincial coordination, with resulting inertia; our fundamental opportunity is the motivation and creativity of our communities.

## References

1   Marche, S. (2007). Professional Development Needs of Graduate Students: Comparing and Contrasting Perspectives. Proceedings of the Administrative Sciences Association of Canada. Halifax, May 24-27. http://www.dalgrad.dal.ca/annualreports/professional_development_original.pdf.

2   OCGS By-Laws and Procedures Governing Appraisals, article 6.4.1. http://ocgs.cou.on.ca/_bin/home/byLaws.cfm.

3   http://www.marsdd.com/mars/Events/Event-Calendar/Ent101.html.

4   http://www.engineering.utoronto.ca/informationfor/graduate/ethics.htm http://www.oise.utoronto.ca/research/rethics.html.

5   Anne McIlroy, (2008, June 20). Scientists get their own Hippocratic oath. *Globe and Mail.* http://www.theglobeandmail.com/servlet/story/RTGAM.20080620.wlethics20/BNStory/specialScienceandHealth/home.

# How Are Graduate Experiences and the Institutional Environment Assessed?

**Suzanne Ortega**
**Provost and Executive Vice President**
**University of New Mexico**

In the white paper entitled "The Project for Scholarly Integrity in Graduate Education: A Framework for Collaborative Action," the Council of Graduate Schools has provided a succinct history of responsible conduct of research (RCR) initiatives. The paper details the forces driving current efforts and presents some very promising ideas on best practices and next steps. I will focus my remarks on just one of the points raised in the paper and then try to trace its implications through to strategies for assessing student learning and institutional climate. From the CGS (2008) framework, the premise is

> Research integrity is not simply an individual value, it is also an institutional value reflected in the culture that is reinforced by the processes in place and the daily decisions of individual researchers, faculty and mentors, campus leaders, and administrative staff.[1]

Let me suggest that this statement represents an important turning point in our thinking about research integrity. It represents a shift from a singular focus on individual values, knowledge, and behavior to the recognition that individual behavior is always socially situated. Specifically, it means that no matter how well we educate our students about the nine core areas of responsible conduct of research, no matter how thoughtful our attempts are to help them enhance ethical decision-making skills, our efforts will fail unless we simultaneously create an institutional culture that reinforces adherence to the highest standards of scholarly integrity. For those of us charged with providing effective individual-level RCR preparation **and** with creating an institutional environment that facilitates and rewards scholarly integrity, the obvious question is how will we know how well we are doing now and how will we measure improvements along the way.

While there is a long way to go, I believe we are making real progress in designing instruments and measurement strategies that capture individual student learning outcomes. In partnership with The Office of Research Integrity and the National Science Foundation, CGS and participating universities such as Old Dominion and University of Oklahoma have developed assessment instruments that will help us understand the effectiveness of our various RCR pedagogical strategies. Furthermore, despite a number of challenges, including those stemming from the under-reporting of incidences of misconduct, we are even making progress at the most macro-level in devising ways of monitoring whether or not our collective RCR efforts are actually improving the national research environment. Surveys such as those conducted by Martinson, Anderson, and deVries (2005) give us baseline estimates of the prevalence of ethical lapses by scientists and, at the national level, offices such as ORI monitor trends in the number of reported ethical violations.[2] At the level of the university, however, our efforts are only beginning. This is where our greatest assessment challenge may lie, but also where we have an important opportunity to leverage changes we are seeing at the level of student learning and research compliance. Let me suggest a couple of assessment strategies that just might work.

First, what would an inventory of university rewards and resource allocation processes reveal about the importance of scholarly integrity in the overall life of the university? Most U.S. universities annually recognize faculty for outstanding contributions to teaching, research, and service. Would an audit of nomination materials show, for example, that contributions to research or teaching ethics is a key selection criteria? Are there specific awards for faculty, postdocs, or graduate students for their work in RCR mentoring? Do tenure and promotion dossiers provide space for candidates and their reviewers to reflect on work done to foster a climate of scholarly integrity in the classroom, lab, or community? Conversely, does language found in faculty by-laws or other university policies explicitly recognize infractions of responsible conduct of research standards as potential grounds for sanction? One could easily imagine an assessment strategy that would chart changes in the overall ethical environment of a university by changes in the number of key processes and resource allocation decisions that included scholarly integrity as one of the award criteria.

A second, and perhaps even more promising strategy, stems from the work that Martinson, Anderson, Crain, and De Vries (2006) have done on perceptions of organizational justice and self-reported misbehaviors[3]. According to these authors, ethical lapses are most likely to occur when individuals believe that 1) professional rewards - publications in peer reviewed journals or receipt of grant funding, for example - are unfairly distributed, and 2) there are few negative consequences, and perhaps even some positive ones, for violating rules of fair play and scholarly integrity. This study uses a survey instrument for assessing perceptions of organizational justice that could be adapted for use on our campuses so that the scholarly environment of classrooms and/or work done in the arts and humanities could also be taken into account. Using this approach (augmented by others no doubt), universities could measure improvements in their ethical climate by documenting an increase in the number of faculty, students, and administrators who 1) believe that they understand the process by which scholarly rewards are distributed, 2) believe that those processes are fair even if the outcomes are not equal, 3) think that most of their colleagues follow the rules, and 4) expect that violations of principles of scholarly integrity will be acted on quickly and with certain negative consequence by the university, professional associations, and governmental agencies.

It seems to me that there are a number of principles implicit in this assessment strategy, including ones that we do not often think about as falling under the rubric of responsible conduct of research. Nevertheless, I would argue that attention to those elements is as essential as that we pay to modules designed to educate our students about data acquisition, conflict of interest, animal welfare, research misconduct, and so on. Broadly writ, these elements are the same as those that underlie doctoral reform initiatives such as Preparing Future Faculty. Specifically, our challenge (and perhaps our moral obligation) is to insure that each of our students understands the standards and the processes by which scholarly work is reviewed by granting agencies and journals, to provide opportunities to develop the skills and the networks that will allow them to successfully navigate those waters, and for those who choose not to play the grants and publication "game," to provide opportunities to prepare for rewarding alternative careers. A truly comprehensive and effective approach to scholarly integrity will, I think, involve integrating our more traditional approaches to RCR education with the full range of doctoral reform initiatives now underway, including those related to Preparing Future Faculty and Doctoral Completion.

## References

1   The Project for Scholarly Integrity in Graduate Education: A Framework for Collaborative Action. (2008). Website of the Council of Graduate Schools, http://www.cgsnet.org/portals/0/pdf/PSI_framework_document.pdf.

2   Martinson, B.C., Anderson, M.S., & De Vries, R. (2005). Scientists Behaving Badly. Nature 435(9): 737-738.

3    Martinson, B.C., Anderson, M.S., Crain, A.L., De Vries, R. (2006). Scientists' Perceptions of Organizational Justice and Self-Reported Misbehaviors. Journal of Empirical Research on Human Research Ethics 1(1): 51-66.

# What Specific Issues Do You Face in Educating a Multicultural Community for Careers in Research?

Christine Keitel-Kreidt
Vice-President
Freie University Berlin

In Germany, we have acknowledged rather late that we were to become a multicultural/ multinational community. In the late 60's Turkish workers were called to Germany because of a lack of working force in this period, but we did not foresee that they would stay, and were not prepared for the fact until becoming aware of major problems recently. The opening of the wall and of all frontiers of the European Community around Germany have increased the population of migrant people in Germany, and today we are faced with the situation that at least 27% of all families with children under 18 years are migrant people. Neither the school system nor the system of higher education and research has taken this new situation into account nor is it prepared to do so.

The population of migrant people is varied, but by far the most are of Turkish origin, next to Russian, Polish, and other Slavic countries, and is not equally distributed within the country and not of the same origin everywhere in Germany. In some big cities like Berlin, Frankfurt and Cologne, the social gap between the German and the migrant – here mostly Turkish - population is very big, in particular concerning access to and success in schooling and higher education. In particular in Berlin, where we face the biggest Turkish community outside Turkey, only a very small percentage of such migrant pupils have/get the chance to enter the gymnasium type of high school, which is the very precondition for reaching higher education; academic-oriented high schools and among migrant students at Freie University Berlin, the Turkish students in majority are female, and there is a surprisingly much bigger group of girls than boys who successfully finish their studies. However, this is surprising at a first glance only: Girls are more successful in German and Foreign languages and when they apply to become teachers; they are not expected to study MINT-subjects, while Turkish boys are considered by their parents more able and successful as future entrepreneurs (craftsmen, dealers, shopowners) for which they do not need higher education. Turkish girls may be considered "better" (more prosperous) and more likely to be married if well educated, and the teaching profession is more valued by Turkish parents than by German ones.

Facing these problems while being concerned with social justice and equal opportunity issues in higher education and research, FUB has started several initiatives that should take into account these general goals:

1.  Specific measures have been set up to care for necessary preconditions that support success in high schools. Being able to speak, learn and teach in more than one language obviously is one major precondition in order to be better able to care of the variety of migrant students. In order to provide easier access to Gymnasium and later to university for more students, we have several international schools in Berlin that use at least two official languages for teaching and learning. Famous in Berlin is the recently set up German-Turkish International School with German and Turkish as the official languages of teaching and learning with equal rights. Patterns for such types of school are numerous in Berlin and some date back to earlier times. Other successful high schools leading to university are the French Lyceum, as a state school with the official languages French and German for teaching and learning founded in 1689; the John F. Kennedy High School with English and German as languages of schooling established after World-war II; the Italian-German High School; the Japanese-German High School, and some private International Schools. These schools contribute to internationalization as well. Some schools offer more than the mostly used languages in their program, and Chinese has become a highly demanded foreign language.

2.  New preconditions have been established that allow better access to university. As all state-run universities have restricted access to all subject areas, additional conditions are used for selection procedures: success /good marks in certain school subjects is the most common additional measure for selection, which means that more success in subjects like MINT-subjects (math, informatics, natural sciences, informatics) and better language skills count as surplus within the admission procedure. To improve teaching and learning in such subjects is therefore an important measure for offering access to university to more students, in particular those from a migrant background. Although the school system generally does not foster the success of girls in such subjects, it is remarkable that Turkish girls have much fewer difficulties coping and engaging

with these subjects in comparison with German girls. What they hesitate to do, however, is to study these subjects as they do not see chances in professional areas where these subjects lead. More substantial information and pre-university-courses to learn about the chances of such subjects are good measures for improving these attitudes.

3. Better formation of teachers to produce more future university students. Increasing diversity and diversity management abilities of teachers in schools and universities, more content knowledge in MINT-subjects, more didactic qualification in all school subjects that support students who have less access and information about their future chances in such subject areas. Additional measures include:

   a) Teaching and studying German as a foreign language to all teachers; encouraging more migrant students to become teachers in German schools to better support migrant children and supervise their success or failure.

   b) Migrant students, in particular Turkish students as well as lower class students for whom the university is a much less familiar place than for German upper class students, have to be supported by a system of mentors and mentoring at university and supervised carefully in their success and progress. In addition, already in high schools, special afternoon group-work is offered, to which parents are invited to participate to learn about in-school and outside-school activities and to acknowledge education as a very important aspect of the future of their children.

   c) Encourage more Turkish teachers to teach in primary schools as well as in high schools, more MINT-Teachers with a migrant background to teach in Gymnasium.

4. More success at university. How to become a researcher? The number of positions that provide research activities is related to the number of scientific projects that are funded. As Freie University has won in the excellence competition, research activities in interesting projects are available to more young researchers and contribute to improvement of their research capacities.

However, success at university is not enough to get more migrant students into research activities and to advise them how to successfully do research. Only if we offer university studies providing both professional (also work-oriented) qualification as well as research qualification, along with a good sense of what research is and what is necessary, possible, encouraging, and fascinating in research in important subject areas, will we be successful in getting more migrant students to become successful researchers. The chance to do research in German universities is very rare for most students; serious introduction and encouragement into research activities is firstly only offered to the few that survive several competitions, and secondly very stressful for many who have to have a job to support themselves while studying. It is still very rare to find Turkish students among young researchers in Berlin, while other incoming foreign students sometimes more easily turn to research while bringing with them positive perceptions and prospective visions. To convey such visions is necessary but often not seriously done.

5.   More success in research capacity building and in developing socially relevant outcomes of research. Increasing diversity and diversity management capacity is strongly related to professional success and the commitment to research. Here we face very different problems internationally, e.g. how to assure students that research is not only determined by companies and laboratories outside universities that are more interested in business and financial success than solving important problems (ex. HIV-related research) and how to convey a general socially determined commitment in research by those who teach and let students work for them.

# Issues in Educating a Multicultural/Multinational Community for Careers in Research

### Fred L. Hall
### Vice-Provost of Graduate Education
### University of Calgary

At the present time at the University of Calgary, there is no university-wide approach to educating graduate students on research ethics or academic integrity. The Faculty of Medicine has a short course that is required for all of its students, offered through its Office of Medical Bioethics. In addition, programs in Nursing and Social Work have some material on professional ethics, but that is not the same as research ethics and academic integrity. Because of the absence of a university-wide approach at Calgary, this paper draws on experience at my previous institution, McMaster University, in Ontario, Canada. The paper describes the approach taken at McMaster to educate a multicultural student body about academic integrity; the reasons for the approach; and alternate approaches that have been considered.

In 2005, McMaster's Graduate Council introduced a new requirement for all incoming graduate students to "ensure uniformity of message" and to communicate to each student at an early time "the priority that McMaster assigns" to academic research integrity and ethics.[1] Each student must attend a two-hour presentation on academic integrity, and pass a short test at the end of the session. (In several respects, this is modeled on the approach to ensuring students know about Workplace Hazardous Materials.) The requirement appears in the form of a course requirement, which appears on the student's transcript:

SGS #101 / Academic Research Integrity and Ethics
This course will introduce incoming graduate students to the standards of academic integrity expected at McMaster. It will provide examples of acceptable and unacceptable practices and will clarify the responsibility and expectations of graduate students with respect to academic integrity. Students will be exposed to the Academic Integrity Policy of McMaster and best practices will be described that will minimize the likelihood of incorrectly attributed work … appearing in their assignments and research records.[2]

This requirement was introduced largely at the instigation of an individual who had served for several years as one of the "Faculty Adjudicators" responsible for dealing with allegations of academic dishonesty against graduate students. Most of the allegations involved plagiarism in written work, in almost all cases against students from countries other than Canada. Invariably, the defense by the students was that they were not aware of the rules in Canada, and that things were done differently in their home country. One example of the extent of the difference, we were told, is that in some countries it is a mark of respect to use extensive passages taken directly from work by a distinguished scientist or author (including one's own professor). Footnoting or other acknowledgment is not expected. In Canada, that action is one of the classic examples of plagiarism, and is unacceptable academic conduct. Clearly something was lacking in the education these students were receiving in coming to a different culture. Introduction of this new requirement was seen as the way to overcome this lack of information.

There were, however, both practical and philosophical concerns with this short course. On the practical side, the course needed to be given to nearly 1,000 students per year. The logistics of confirming attendance, administering the test, and marking it afterward were all difficult, as was finding a lecture theatre large enough to accommodate the group each term. On the philosophical side, there was concern that students who had come through a Canadian or similar undergraduate education would find it insulting to be told this same information again, and would treat it as a joke, thereby undermining the effect it was intended to have for the non-Canadian students. We debated the possibility of making the course mandatory only for students from other cultures or countries, even going so far as to consult with the university's Human Rights Officer to determine if doing so would contravene the Ontario Human Rights Code.[3] The response was that since the course was intended to overcome a shortcoming rather than to penalize those individuals, it would be legal to limit the group that was required to take it. We remained uncomfortable with that option however, and as of the 2008-09 Calendar it is clear that the course is still mandatory for all incoming students.

A few other points were recently made by an individual involved with the course:[4]

- Although there are benefits to a Faculty (or College or School)-based offering, which can be more focused on the issues specific to a particular discipline, it is harder to achieve uniformity of message when a variety of such sessions occur.
- A benefit of including all students (not just international ones) is that all students become similarly informed about the local graduate rules and procedures.

- Incoming international faculty are frequently also ill-informed of such issues.
- Many of the students required to repeat the course are unable to grasp or answer the nature of the questions on the test because of weak English language skills.
- It is not clear whether SGS101 has reduced graduate student dishonesty.
- A volunteer faculty member from each large cultural group on campus could meet with students from that group and act as an "academic integrity cultural mentor."

The issues that this example illustrates, but does not necessarily solve, are the following.

- Students arrive at graduate school with a variety of previous experience and knowledge about what constitutes academic integrity and research ethics.
- To provide no education or training upon entry to graduate school places one set of students at risk of contravening rules or expectations of which they are understandably ignorant.
- To require for all students uniform entry-level information about the basic aspects of academic integrity and plagiarism risks having the exercise not taken seriously by those students who were already educated under those expectations.
- Treating students who come from these different backgrounds differently in terms of the education about academic integrity required of them risks being accused of discrimination.

## Notes and References

1 McMaster University School of Graduate Studies Calendar, 2008-2009, p. 222, as found at http://www.mcmaster.ca/graduate/grad_calendar.pdf, 1August 2008.

2 Ibid. The # symbol simply indicates that the course length is less than a full term.

3 http://www.e-laws.gov.on.ca/html/Statutes/English/elaws_statutes_90h19_e.htm.

4 Thanks to Douglas Welch for these points.

# IV. EMERGING "BEST PRACTICES" IN RESEARCH AND SCHOLARLY INTEGRITY

## Summary of Presentations and Group Discussion

For the fourth session of the Global Leaders Summit, participants were asked to describe promising new practices their institutions are using to address issues of scholarly integrity. The discussion covered practical approaches to a range of topics, including the development of training programs in scholarly integrity for faculty and graduate students, the shaping of institutional values, and the creation of positive (preventative) programs to respond to specific ethical issues.

The first set of papers addressed the general problem of defining institutional ethical obligations in research ethics through a specific topic—**conflicts of interest or commitment**. As the presenters showed, conflicts of interest are ethical problems that require universities to affirm their commitments to using research to promote the public good and to ensuring that graduate education is not compromised by special interests that may arise in research projects involving industry. The papers for this part of the session stressed the need for transparency of guidelines governing situations where conflicts of interest or commitment might occur: **Adriano De Maio** of the University of Milan gave emphasis to institutional guidelines for regulating relationships between universities and industry partners; **Eva Pell** of the Pennsylvania State University and **Jeffery Gibeling** of the University of California, Davis, described their institutions' work to protect graduate students involved in faculty research;[1] and Dr. Gibeling discussed the ways in which international collaboration among universities governed by different policies requires administrators and researchers to become more aware of different local requirements as well as international agreements governing research.

Building upon previous discussions of graduate education, the group also considered **new curricular resources** for training graduate students in the responsible conduct of research. Many participants noted that while the widespread availability of internet technology creates a higher incidence of plagiarism, this technology also offers new ways of educating students about scholarly integrity. It was also observed that online tools for detecting plagiarism, such as "Turnitin," can serve to educate as well as to monitor, since they often create in students a greater awareness of standards for originality and responsible citation. A second form of technology was introduced by **Bryan Noe** in his presentation on the use of video vignettes at the University of Alabama at Birmingham. Dr. Noe explained that the "interactive" nature of these videos, which depict students attempting to resolve various ethical dilemmas related to research, helps viewers become more aware of limitations in their own knowledge about research ethics. A number of participants added that this form of technology also helps students and faculty to identify with a character encountering an ethical dilemma and reflect about how they might act in a similar situation.

The discussion of graduate education also shed light on the importance of making education in scholarly integrity an integral part of a graduate student's program. **Greg Koski** of Massachusetts General Hospital emphasized this point in his presentation on new curricular approaches: universities must demonstrate the importance of ethics training by making it a fundamental part of their curricula. A number of other presenters suggested strategies for giving special weight to ethics training. **William Russel** of Princeton University described a new online assessment tool that is an integral part of each graduate student's program; this tool has the potential to reveal, through a structured dialogue between graduate students and their mentors, weaknesses in a graduate student's progress in the Ph.D. program. **Anthony Yeh** of the University of Hong Kong also emphasized early intervention, explaining that his university makes available a range of resources about ethical guidelines at student orientation and requires students to sign a declaration that they understand the rules of ethical scholarship.

In the last session of the panel, on the **ethical and psychological implications of research on sensitive topics**, participants gave extended attention to the ethical obligations of universities in overseeing human subjects research. Rather than focusing exclusively on protecting the rights of research subjects, the presenters for this section shed new light on the perspectives of researchers, which can be dynamically linked to those of their subjects. The group considered two main strategies for ensuring that projects on sensitive topics are conducted in an ethical way. First, **Yvonne Carter** of the Warwick Medical School focused on the importance of defining institutional values, and training researchers to identify conflicting values, when conducting research on sensitive topics. Research models must integrate pressing research questions with patient values, she noted, so that research projects harmonize the perspectives and values of all groups (patients, researchers, organizations).

Second, Dr. Carter and **Robyn Owens** of the University of Western Australia discussed the obligations of universities to researchers who study potentially stress-inducing topics. Both presenters observed that universities can reduce the chance that researchers will experience a psychological form of occupational stress by determining the factors that contribute to the stress levels of researchers and identifying resources to support them, such as training and counseling services.

As in the previous session, the conversation about "best practices" reflected the view that universities must work to clarify the ethical responsibilities of different groups, whether these groups are divided according to roles within the university (faculty, students, administration) or according to discipline or type of research. Making visible these obligations at every level can serve to improve the confidence of various groups in the transparency and fairness of an institution's ethical policies.

## Notes

1   Eva Pell and Jeffery Gibeling were unable to present at the session, but their papers were made available to participants and are included in this volume.

# Conflict of Interest and Classified Research: Two Challenges for Graduate Education

Eva J. Pell
Senior Vice President for Research and
Dean of the Graduate School
Pennsylvania State University

Conflict of interest is a subject that has been in the news a lot lately. But there is nothing new about the notion of conflict of interest. When an individual is involved in an endeavor and the outcome of that activity will impact his or her interests, there is an inherent conflict of interest. Just because a conflict of interest exists does not mean that the outcome will automatically be sinister. However, the potential for malfeasance exists and at the very least, the appearance of conflict of interest can be harmful to the associated institution.

The conflicts of interest which have received the greatest attention have been those surrounding medical research. In those cases faculty have conducted research and/or clinical trials on therapies in which they also had significant financial interest, either through consulting, or because of direct investments by the interested companies in their research programs. The risk in these medically-related examples has been a national focus of concern, but conflicts of interest can also take other forms.

Universities are being actively encouraged to develop their intellectual property; most state governments view universities as an important source of economic development. A favorite approach for pulling intellectual property out of universities is to form spin-out companies that can take early innovative ideas and develop them until they ripen into profitable concerns. Most universities recognize that faculty should not serve as Presidents or CEOs of these spin-out companies, and often they have policies that prevent faculty from assuming such roles. Faculty rarely have the business knowledge to be effective in these roles nor do they have the time that must be committed to allow the company to achieve success. But often spin-out companies cannot be successful without the scientific input provided by the faculty member. As the originators and inventors of the intellectual property that form the foundation for these companies, the faculty must be engaged in roles like Chief Technology Officer or Consultant to help further develop the technology. Often the spin-out company will contract with the faculty to do follow-on research, again because of unique capabilities that he or she has to offer.

Graduate students can become the unwitting subjects of a conflict of interest in a number of ways. Often graduate students are enlisted to help faculty members in research activities directly or indirectly associated with a faculty member's entrepreneurial activities. The faculty member may invite the graduate student to work in the company. This employment could represent an opportunity for a student. If funding in the faculty member's research program has become less available and an assistantship has "dried up," work in the company could be a source of income for the student; working in the company could also lead to postgraduate employment. Alternatively, a company could contract with a faculty member to conduct research in his or her laboratory and graduate students could be asked to provide assistance in running some key experiments for which they have particular skills or knowledge. A graduate student may feel obligated to respond to the request of his or her mentor, even if the work requested is not connected to the student's research.

Such arrangements are fraught with potential conflicts of interest for the faculty member. The graduate student may not be interested in diverting his or her efforts from the dissertation research; but if the student refuses to work with the faculty member, will there be repercussions? If the student agrees to assist the faculty member with his or her company, will that effort delay completion of his or her degree? Or if the graduate student helps conduct some research that is funded by the company, is there the risk that publication will be delayed or prevented to protect the company's proprietary interests?

It is imperative that universities have guidelines that protect the interests of graduate students in these cases. Conflicts of interest of this sort are manageable. But they must be disclosed up front before a student is approached. With suitable oversight and monitoring it should be possible for students to have the opportunity to choose to participate or not, and to participate at a level that positively affects their graduate experience without distracting them from the primary goal of completing their education. Graduate students should not be engaged in research that prevents the free exchange of ideas. And most importantly, any disclosure of conflicts of interest on the part of the faculty member must be transparent to the graduate student before he or she is enlisted to support such activities.

In summary, graduate students' interests are protected when well developed conflict of interest policies are in place; conflicts must be disclosed, and plans for resolution and management must be developed. Penn State University has published guidelines related to resolution of conflicts of interest.[1] The following principles are cited in the Guidelines for the Development of a Conflict of Interest Resolution Plan and reiterated here:

- Graduate student thesis research should be directed to unencumbered publication in the open literature. The corollary holds; graduate student research should not be directed to the financial benefit of a university employee, especially the student's thesis advisor.
- "[…] rigid safeguards must be instituted to ensure that the graduate student does not even perceive that graduate work has been affected by the Company-student employment relationship."

Classified research presents a special challenge for graduate education and particularly for graduate education in an international context. Classified research is conducted at a subset of U.S. universities. To conduct classified research, universities must have systems that allow researchers to secure appropriate federal clearances. Classified research can only be conducted in facilities that have the appropriate security, thus insuring that access to the research is only obtained by those with necessary clearance and also those with a "need to know." Classified research is publication restricted; as such, no research can be published unless cleared by the cognate sponsor. Because the workforce in many classified areas is graying rapidly, it is both an opportunity and an imperative for some graduate students to be educated in this environment. Securing necessary clearances is time consuming and obtaining such approvals can be an asset to a student with career aspirations for which a clearance is a prerequisite. That said, the conditions of classified research represent a challenge for graduate education. First, graduate students must be able to publish their research, so it would be difficult for dissertation research to be classified. In laboratories where a great deal of classified research is conducted, it is sometimes possible to carve out an element of that research that can be published. In such cases graduate students may be able to work on classified research projects.

A second problem arises because only U.S. citizens can work on classified projects. So, if a professor who conducts classified research also has research projects which are unclassified, it will be challenging to have a blend of U.S. citizens and international students working in the same laboratory. Technically it would be possible to do so, by providing a space for the classified research that was removed from the rest of the laboratory. However, the usual free exchange of ideas and sharing of research problems would be somewhat stifled by two populations of graduate students.

Classified research will rarely, if ever, be a major activity in graduate education at a single institution. However, if carefully managed, the ability for graduate students to be involved in classified research can provide a valuable education path for certain students.

## References

1   Pennsylvania State Research Office, Guidelines for the Development
    of a Conflict of Interest Resolution Plan and the Preparation of a
    Memorandum of Understanding (1995).   http://www.research.psu.
    edu/osp/PSU/Toolbox/coi2fill.pdf.   Sections 8-9 focus on student
    involvement.

# Emerging "Best Practices" Research and Scholarly Integrity: Conflict of Interest and Conflict of Commitment in University/Industry Partnerships

Adriano De Maio
President (IreR)
University of Milan

In approaching this question, we must subdivide universities (or departments inside a university) into two classes: to the first one belong high-level technical universities or departments; to the second, all the other universities or departments. Even if conflicts of interest and/or commitment concern both groups, the first one is more deeply implicated. For this reason we will focus our attention specifically on the first group.

The success of a technical university depends not only on the quality of research (and for evaluating quality, one can adopt the usual scientific indicators), but also on the relevance of the applications derived from the research itself (and the number of patents is only one indicator, and not the most important, that can be used). The "quality" of applications affects educational evaluation at all three levels and it is also a key factor in attracting talented people: scientists, investigators, and professors, as well as brilliant students who want either to be future scientists and/or high technical and professional-skilled people with real chances for a managerial career. The quality of applications also attracts funds from industry and charities and grants from public or private funds.

For this reason research strategy can follow two paths, which are synergistically and strictly linked to one another. The first one is concerned with "curiosity driven research" in which resources are distributed following "quality priorities": the problem consists in defining priorities or relevance when comparing different scientific fields because in many cases it is impossible to find quality indicators that are appropriate for all fields. The decision is a political one and there is a risk of forcing the decision via some industrial or academic push.

The European Research Council (ERC) follows this way and the approach is more or less followed also at a state and at a regional level. In this case an international comparison and evaluation can also be useful. In principle, if this strategy is adopted by a university, there will not be any conflict with industry; on the contrary, this strategy is very important for industrial development because new fields of research and, consequently, new educational curricula, could anticipate new industrial frontiers. But a conflict could be generated with respect to educational curricula because industries, and specifically SMEs, very often want curricula targeted to present skill necessities, while research universities define curricula according to, or mainly to, future needs. Universities must be proactive not only in defining research activities but also in outlining educational activities. In addition, there is a delay, not a short one, between the time when a new curriculum is designed and the time when new skilled people will be on the market. But we cannot ignore conflicts inside the academy itself, especially when (as in the Italian situation), there are strong disciplinary academic lobbies and it is very difficult to overcome disciplinary barriers—for instance, in defining a nanomedicine curriculum, in which medical science, physics, chemistry, computer science, mathematics, biology, and engineering must be linked together. Paradoxically, in cases like this, industry might be a strong allied partner and not an enemy of an innovative academy. But there are other potential conflicts regarding some results obtained through curiosity-driven research. The first one can be found "inside" a single investigator: results must be written in a scientific paper and distributed to all, (this will permit a faster academic career) or can be used for a patent (and some money could be expected). In some countries (in Italy, for instance. and, more or less throughout the E.U.), if a result is published, it cannot be patented in any way. The second "conflict" is inside the university and concerns the rights of property (for instance, what must be the share between investigator, department and university and for what time; what are the internal rules and bylaws between the shareholders, etc.). The third one regards the "use" of the patent: licensing, selling, a new company (spin-off) and this problem is generated if these kinds of rules are not decided in a general way, before patenting. In this case we can say that there is a conflict between university and "potential company."

The second method is what we call "focused research," that is, defining a set of research projects within a well-defined objective (regarding, for instance, health, environment, energy, food etc.) without any constraints on the scientific or technological approach used. Usually a network of different actors, and not only of disciplines, is requested: the commitment (in many cases a public administration), the research centers (universities, etc), industry and finance. The research results must be at a pre-competitive stage, one in which all the results are published, due also to the fact that monetary resources are given by a public administration (the E.U., central or local government). This is the case of Europoean FPs and of many state and regional programs. Industry and finance are partners because a real feasibility analysis is needed either in productivity or in economic sustainability. The definition of a specific objective (target) to be reached implies that ethical problems are solved or, at least, explicitly discussed (and also approved by scientists and by popular consensus, both nationally and internationally).

This consideration gives us a way of eliminating or, at least, reducing many possible ethical conflicts between industry and universities even in cases involving other types of contracts and grants. Each grant must have a clear statement on objectives to be obtained and constraints to be respected. These objectives and constraints must be examined by an "ethical committee", both "ex ante" for grant approval (defining the purpose of the grant) and "ex post" to observe obtained results. This rule is not yet in force; now it is being studied and the same procedure could also be followed for the so-called "open laboratories" open to many different users, among which there are also industries. Of course constraints that are to be discussed regard also IP. In this view, "classified research" is only a specific case, even if it is highly sensitive. Ethical committees must also be "classified" and investigators must be acquainted and must accept, preliminarily, all the rules.

In closing, a very brief consideration: in the past, agreements between universities and industry produced benefits for the two actors that were greater than resulting difficulties and problems. Now ethical sensibilities are more widely diffused and raise issues that in the recent past were not perceived as concerns, including the care of the environment, the wasting of resources, etc. The approach that is now studied is not, of course, the only one possible, but we must experiment with it.

# Conflict of Interest and Conflict of Commitment in Graduate Education

### Jeffery C. Gibeling
### Dean of Graduate Studies
### University of California, Davis

Modern research universities have a vested interest in ensuring that research results obtained by their faculty and graduate students serve the public good. Toward this goal, universities have developed mechanisms to support faculty efforts to transfer research discoveries from the laboratory to industry, often by encouraging and assisting faculty who wish to start their own companies based on research conducted at the university. In the United States, these technology transfer activities were made possible by the Bayh-Dole Act (1980) in which recipients of federal funding were granted rights to retain research results and given the responsibility of transferring technology to application. The act also specified that income from the transfer of technology was to be shared with the inventor. There have been many successful technology transfer activities since the act was adopted, and the most successful have spawned entire new industries.

More recently, some universities have developed entrepreneurship programs that are designed to train graduate students and postdoctoral scholars to think creatively about how to take the results of their research out into the business world. Participants in these programs are encouraged to develop strategies to commercialize their research; are introduced to the concepts of venture capital and marketing; and may be provided with direct opportunities to interact with business development professionals. In this way, universities have opened a second pathway for commercialization of research results while preparing students and postdoctoral scholars to enhance the competitiveness of science and technology within the country.

By promoting the transfer of ideas and technology to commercial activity, universities strengthen their base of public support and investment; stimulate economic development and contribute to social well-being within their regional communities; and capitalize on their large investments in research infrastructure through patent and licensing revenue. Of course, success in these undertakings requires that universities have clear policies that – at least partially - assign patent rights to the institutions, that they have processes for disclosing inventions and that they have licensing strategies to enable resources to flow back to the institution.

However, promoting technology transfer and entrepreneurship naturally leads to conflicts of interest and conflicts of commitment in which an individual's private interests may compromise or have the appearance of compromising his or her professional actions. Faculty who form companies are naturally anxious for these enterprises to succeed technically and financially. Similarly, students who seek to transfer their research discoveries from the laboratory to product development or service applications through entrepreneurship programs have a vested interest in their ventures. Conflicts of interest are first financial in nature, as there are inevitable challenges in separating university business from company business. Having actively established programs that inherently create conflicts of interest, universities must have policies and procedures for minimizing or managing those conflicts since they cannot be avoided. Such policies typically begin with disclosure of the conflict to all interested parties (especially by faculty to students), provide for independent review of the disclosure, and limit decisions that can be made by participants to the extent necessary to ensure that actions are not colored by their conflicting interests. An essential part of an effective conflict of interest management strategy is a review board that is available to provide impartial analysis of the proposed safeguards.

Looking beyond financial matters, these situations also give rise to what might be termed academic conflict of interest or conflict of judgment. For example, a faculty member who has formed a start-up company may intentionally or unintentionally influence the research being undertaken by a graduate student or postdoctoral scholar at the university in a direction that benefits company interests, thereby subverting the academic interests of the student or postdoc. Similarly, when the student or postdoc is undertaking an entrepreneurial activity, his or her research direction may be inappropriately biased by an interest in seeing the commercial venture succeed. Academic conflict of interest is a difficult form of conflict to manage, as any efforts undoubtedly confront issues of academic freedom.

Finally, faculty, graduate students and postdoctoral scholars with outside interests in promoting a commercial activity may also develop a conflict of effort or commitment. That is, they may spend time engaged in an entrepreneurial activity at the expense of time due to the university. To the extent that university activities are separable from outside professional activities, universities may rely on explicit policies that limit the time that faculty spend on such activities. Rarely, however, do universities have similar guidelines that limit the outside professional activities of graduate students or postdoctoral scholars, perhaps because of the difficulties of implementing such policies.

Turning to graduate education in an international context, the various forms of conflict of interest can be managed within the traditional model of graduate education in which international students are fully enrolled and clearly subject to all university policies with respect to patents, licensing, conflict of interest, etc. The management strategies are especially clear if the student or postdoc is employed in a research position at the university. However, emerging models of international graduate education open new challenges in this area. Universities throughout the world are exploring and entering into strategic partnerships involving graduate education. Key elements of these partnerships include research exchanges, in which a student earning a degree from one partner institution conducts research at another partner institution for a significant period of time (for example, 6 months to 1 year). Such sandwich programs present new challenges in managing conflicts of interest and commitment, as well as ownership of intellectual property, because the partner institutions may have different policies. Similar challenges arise in joint and dual degree programs in which students conduct research at both partner institutions.

As noted earlier, many institutions have patent policies that define the interests of the researcher and the institution in any discovery that derives from research conducted at the institution. Visiting researchers, particularly those in a student status who are not employed by or enrolled in the university, may find their work to be governed by two, perhaps competing, patent and licensing policies from the home and host institutions. The researcher then potentially suffers an academic conflict of interest and a conflict of commitment. Thus, it is imperative that international exchange agreements involving graduate students include explicit descriptions of how authorship and intellectual property matters are to be managed in order to avoid potential conflicts. Furthermore, a primary motivation for developing international collaborations is to better understand both the research and the research culture of a partner country. To ensure success, students from different countries and cultures need to understand the local regulations and cultures with regard to conflict of interest and conflict of commitment as a core element of their international research experience.

# Ethics and Professionalism in Graduate Education: Innovative Approaches and Evaluation of Effectiveness

**Greg Koski**
**Associate Professor of Anesthesia**
**Massachusetts General Hospital**

Intermittently, media accounts of disturbing unprofessional misconduct by scientists underscores widespread and growing concern that existing approaches to training scientists may lack sufficient emphasis on the core values that set the moral compass of scientists and preserve both the integrity of science and public trust in the scientific endeavor. Several institutions and organizations have recently initiated efforts to better understand the issues, although they are not new, and to develop more effective approaches. The issues are well presented and discussed in the 2002 report from the Institute of Medicine of the National Academies of Science.[1]

Many graduate students in the sciences have been introduced to these topics and concerns through recommended readings, such as the excellent book *On Being a Scientist: Responsible Conduct in Research*, now in its third edition,[2] and through courses on "responsible conduct of research" offered by most institutions receiving funding from the National Institutes of Health or the National Science Foundation after a requirement for directed education in these topics became a pre-condition for funding of graduate training grants. While many of these efforts have produced high-quality programs that have undoubtedly had impact, hopefully more positive than negative, their being "offered" as a requirement on weekends or evenings as an adjunct to the existing training programs in science and methodology frequently leaves students with the perception that they were an afterthought—which of course, they were. Indeed, one can well argue that anything worth learning would be offered as part of the core curriculum of graduate education.

Obviously, and ironically, the exclusion of these topics from that core curriculum is not attributable to the students, but to their teachers and administrators who developed their training programs, and this exclusion reflects their priorities and the needs they perceive students to have. The importance of one's mentor and the values and priorities conveyed to students by their mentors cannot be overstated. Graduate students are strongly influenced by their mentors and the behaviors displayed by the individuals they respect most. A recent survey of academic faculty at various ranks suggests that graduate students and trainees are perhaps even more idealistic than their colleagues at more advanced faculty ranks. This observation may reflect a serious systemic problem, namely that the system that we have created not only fails to adequately provide training in these critically important areas, but in fact, may actually undermine the very norms, values and practices we would hope to instill in young scientists.

Our challenge then is to identify and implement the most effective and efficient ways to incorporate training in responsible conduct, ethics and professionalism into our education system for graduate education, and to develop approaches for assessing the effectiveness of these programs. Of course, any form of evaluation requires that the desired goals be specified so that outcomes can be assessed. A working group convened two years ago by Dr. Martha Gray, Director of the Harvard-MIT Program in Health Sciences and Technology, considered these issues and developed a useful framework for consideration. Sharing the concerns stated above, that committee concluded that to the fullest extent possible, education in ethics, responsible conduct and professionalism in science should be integrated into every course offering within the program so as to take advantage of what might best be called "teachable moments," those times when the discussion of the ethical dimensions of a topic arise naturally, such as the ethical concerns that might arise when an engineer believes that a design for a new building is inherently dangerous, or a discussion in a course on renal pathophysiology of the ethics of procuring kidneys for transplantation from executed prisoners as a means of dealing with the shortage of suitable organ donors. One can easily envision a statistics course that takes on the ethical issues associated with data manipulation and presentation.

This integrated approach depends upon 'embedding' critical education and discussion of ethical issues within the regular curriculum and reinforcement of these issues by mentors longitudinally through the continuum of graduate education. The biggest hurdle to be overcome, sadly, is the need to first develop faculty who are properly prepared to rigorously address these areas and to incorporate them into their courses. While this approach poses a challenge, it also poses a very real opportunity to inculcate and reinforce these values among members of the upper-level faculty, something that can hardly be detrimental. One can also envision coordination of this modified curriculum with special lectures, seminars, awards programs and fellowships offered to further reinforce and acknowledge the importance of ethics issues and integrity in the conduct of science and the pursuit and dissemination of knowledge.

One would hope that upon completion of training, every graduate would be able to:

1)  Recognize an ethical dilemma or challenge to scientific integrity when it arises;
2)  Analyze the issue with appropriate reference to ethical principles and/or applicable laws and regulations;
3)  Formulate an appropriate plan for dealing with the issues;
4)  Execute that plan, and;
5)  Internalize the lessons learned from the experience.

Clearly, one would hope that all graduate faculty would also be able do this and teach their students to do so, and while we may assume this to be the case, that contention must be empirically evaluated.

At first glance, it would not appear that novel strategies or methodologies are needed to conduct assessments of these goals, either individually or collectively—the question is whether we have the will to do so. Certainly, essay examinations have long been used effectively to make similar assessments, and those ought to work in these subject areas as well, but one can also easily envision expanding the comprehensive oral examinations given to doctoral students to incorporate these topics in an integrated way, just as they were taught throughout the integrated curriculum. In the final analysis, all of this boils down to ensuring that the culture of scholarship and the institutions where our scholars will be taught fully and unequivocally embrace integrity of scholarship and science as our highest priority.

## References

1  Integrity in Scientific Research: Creating an Environment That Promotes Responsible Conduct (2002). Washington, DC: National Academies Press, http://www.nap.edu/catalog.php?record_id=10430.

2  On Being a Scientist: Responsible Conduct in Research (2006). Washington, DC: National Academies Press.

# Novel Approaches to Expanding and Assessing RCR Education for Graduate Students

**Bryan D. Noe, Dean of the Graduate School**
**Jeffrey Engler,[1] Associate Dean of the Graduate School**
**The University of Alabama at Birmingham (UAB)**

## I. Background and Institutional Context

In the early 1990s, UAB developed a course, "Principles of Scientific Integrity" (GRD 717), which is now mandatory for all graduate students in the biomedical sciences. More than 100 students take this course every year. In response to an increased focus on RCR for the bioscience graduate students at UAB, the Center for Ethics and Values in the Sciences (EVIS) was established in 1998. The Center is led by Philosophy professors Kincaid and Vollmer and is focused on broad value questions in the sciences, not just bioethics. The Center serves as a focal point both on campus and nationally for discussion of value issues in science. The major activities of the Center are sponsoring an annual national conference, administration of the GRD 717 course, ongoing research in ethics education, and presentation of short workshops in research ethics for predoctoral and postdoctoral trainees. The Center is active statewide through collaborations with other universities and nationally through extramurally-funded activities with the HHS Office of Research Integrity. The Center has produced several nationally recognized videos in areas of RCR education, including a DVD on mentoring ("In the Lab: Students and Mentors Behind the Scenes"[2] and a video case study on image manipulation ("Research Integrity in Image Processing").[3]

## II. Expansion of RCR Education into Other Disciplines

One of our goals is to develop RCR educational tools that are relevant to many disciplines. Recently, using funds from a CGS/NSF grant, we expanded RCR educational initiatives into both the School of Engineering and the School of Natural Sciences and Mathematics (NSM).

We set out to accomplish three specific goals:
- Engage faculty and students in the discussion of RCR issues on a continuing basis.

- Develop short video vignettes to dramatize case studies.
- Use assessment tools for measuring the development of ethical reasoning skills.

Motivating factors include:
- Broadening consideration of ethical values within the institution.
- Increasing awareness of the reasons for compliance with professional research standards.
- Educating students, faculty, and staff about the consequences of research misconduct.

## III. Implementation

We used the framework of the GRD 717 course to design new activities/ modules/case studies that would be more focused on issues faced by faculty and students in the natural sciences, mathematics, and engineering disciplines. A group of seven faculty and seven graduate students from these STEM disciplines was assembled to identify RCR issues that often confront faculty and students in their respective areas. From these discussions three case studies evolved.

Video production: We have developed two videos based on the proposed case studies; one deals with plagiarism ("Amanda's Dilemma") and the other with reporting research misconduct ("Whistle Blower"). We are currently testing a teaching strategy developed by Dr. Vollmer, "Query-Videoclip-Query" (QVQ). This approach builds discussion questions of an ethical issue into the video itself. After viewing the video, a facilitated discussion then centers on how to resolve an ethical dilemma. We are examining whether this approach engages students in a high-level discussion, and whether the video enables instructors to prompt students to identify what ethical guidelines should be applied. An important aspect of this approach is that students are actively engaged in discussion of the problem with a facilitator and with each other. Engaging in an interactive discussion is an essential part of the learning process which, experience suggests, is an instructional modality superior to an online tutorial.

## IV. Efficacy Assessment

To engage students in a discussion of Scholarly Integrity (SI) issues, Dr. Jeffrey Engler and other members of the Graduate School staff have created a workshop titled "Avoiding Plagiarism." This workshop has been presented to groups totaling more than 300 undergraduate or graduate students who are studying in various disciplines on the UAB campus. The "Amanda's Dilemma" video was used to introduce students to specific issues of plagiarism. The students are then asked to determine whether a panel of short written scenarios represent plagiarism or not. This exercise reveals the level of students' understanding and provides an opportunity for them to become more well-informed. Post-workshop assessments indicate that students find that the scenarios presented in the workshop increase their understanding of plagiarism in ways that they had not previously considered. To expand the assessment of efficacy, in workshops to be developed, we will ask students to complete a brief questionnaire that deals with the topic to be addressed prior to viewing a video and participating in the subsequent discussion. They will then be asked to complete the same questionnaire after participating in the discussion. The "Pre" and "Post" workshop responses will be compared to determine whether participating in the workshop resulted in an enhanced level of understanding. As this approach is expanded to additional workshop sessions on other scholarly integrity topics, a set of questionnaires will have been developed which can then be integrated into an exit survey which all students are asked to complete at the time of degree conferral. The results from the latter analysis will allow an assessment of long-term retention.

As we strive to incorporate this educational approach into the regular curriculum we will consider implementing the **Trilogy** model developed by Jolly et al.as the theoretical framework for assessment.[4] For the **Engagement** component we will expect students to demonstrate an orientation to integrity issues that includes awareness, motivation and interest. The expectation for the **Capacity** component will be that students possess the acquired knowledge and skills necessary to participate effectively in discussions of ethical decision-making. To fulfill the **Continuity** criterion, it will be important to develop continuing programmatic opportunities, material resources, and guidance designed to support increased understanding of issues of scholarly integrity by graduate students. For this approach to be effective, both pre-engagement and follow-up surveys must be used. Results will be summarized with comparisons made to identify significant discrepancies, using non-parametric tests, and to determine levels of student engagement with descriptive statistics. Capacity and Continuity will be assessed by comparing the follow-up survey data at the time of degree conferral to baseline survey data to identify changes in perceptions and the impact of the instructional modules on the target population.

# V. Challenges

Because we are in the initial stages of integrating RCR education into the graduate curriculum for the Schools of Engineering and of NSM, it is too early in the process to gauge how successful this initiative will be. Using the Engineering and NSM focus groups to identify issues has been successful in engaging students and faculty in discussion of responsible conduct and in deciding what topics to emphasize in RCR training activities. As a result, we have begun to develop useful tools. Development of the case study videos is labor intensive but results from the testing we have completed to date indicate that the approach is effective. However, a concern is how to effectively integrate video materials and case studies into the classroom, or how to use them for continuing education to provide ongoing exposure to RCR issues. This will involve engaging faculty as presenters, some of whom may not be adequately prepared to lead an effective discussion on RCR issues. Getting faculty buy-in and providing training sessions for those faculty members who become committed to the process will be required. It is understood that any attempt to embed ongoing education on scholarly integrity into the fabric of an academic institution will take time to mature. However, we remain committed to expanding RCR education into all disciplines at UAB and recognize that accomplishing our goals will require a long-term effort.

## Notes and References

1  Dr. Engler is listed as co-author of this paper because he is the Graduate School staff member who is primarily responsible for the development of the RCR initiatives and educational tools which are being utilized at UAB.

2  http://ori.dhhs.gov/education/products/rcr_mentoring.shtml.

3  http://www.uab.edu/researchintegrityandimages.

4  Jolly, E., Campbell, P. B., & Perlman, L. (2004). *Engagement, Capacity and Continuity: A Trilogy for Student Success*, GE Foundation.

# Emerging "Best Practices" for Research and Scholarly Integrity

**William B. Russel**
**Dean of the Graduate School**
**Princeton University**

The Graduate School and related units on campus strive to complement the rigorous academic preparation that our Ph.D. students receive in their departments and programs with the professional skills required for successful careers in the academic, corporate, government, and non-profit worlds. For this purpose we envision a multi-staged approach to acquaint students with teaching, communications, and leadership skills; issues of conflict of interest and commitment; the many aspects of research and scholarly integrity; strategies for mentoring students or employees; and the ethical framework to deal with unexpected situations that lie ahead. To accomplish this requires a series of activities at both the departmental and school level that are integrated into or at least complementary to the academic program. We feel that every graduate student needs this, though somewhat less so the humanists, to facilitate their graduate education and prepare them for the complex, difficult, but interesting terrain in their careers beyond graduation.

Some "best practices" exist currently at Princeton, as at other major research universities. Best established are the half-semester courses on responsible conduct of research taught on most campuses since the initial mandate from the National Institutes of Health. One exemplar is the course taught for a number of years by Harold T. Shapiro, president emeritus and professor of economics and public affairs, Woodrow Wilson School 599, "Research Ethics and Scientific Integrity" for social scientists, especially demographers. His first three-hour session frames the moral and ethical perspectives through a discussion of moral philosophy, with subsequent sessions addressing Normative Standards; Formalizing Ethical Research Practice; Learning, Mentoring, Teaching, and Relationships; Responsibilities to Peers; and Scientists' Responsibilities, Constraints, and Conflicts. Readings and actual case studies inform the discussion in each session. A final paper challenges the students to envision their future career and the ethical dilemmas they might encounter. Other courses include Molecular Biology 561, "Scientific Integrity in the Practice of Molecular Biology," with Professor Lee Silver; and Psychology 591a, "Ethical Issues in Scientific Research" and 591b,

"Neuroethics," with Professor Charles Gross, which have similar formats but with content appropriate to the field. Syllabi, reading lists, and case studies for such courses are readily available from a number of universities, the Office of Research Integrity, and through reports of the Council of Graduate Schools.

Another best practice that is well established many places is represented at Princeton by the McGraw Center for Teaching and Learning. In addition to the central focus on teaching, by graduate students and faculty, and learning, on the part of undergraduates and graduate students, these units also assume responsibility for developing future faculty through short courses such as *Becoming a Colleague: Thinking Like a Pro* and *Prof 101: Entering the Professoriate*. The Center also houses the English Language Program, which is "committed to helping non-native English speaking graduate students become fully integrated into the academic community at Princeton." At Harvard, the Derek Bok Center for Teaching and Learning offers professorial advice through a video on *Professional Conduct, a Tip-Sheet on Writing Your First Letter of Recommendation*, a Junior Faculty Institute, and others. Neither at Princeton nor at Harvard do these activities presently incorporate programming on scholarly integrity, but each provides an opportunity for integrating appropriate facets of scholarly integrity into well-accepted components of the educational process.

A third best practice is represented at Princeton by Molecular Biology 500, An Introduction to Laboratory Research, designed to teach basic research techniques in the discipline *and* introduce relevant RCR issues, such as data and image handling and manipulation and publication practices and authorship protocols, to first-year graduate students. This course will be held the month before opening exercises in the Fall for eight hours each day. This new course stands before and complements the current course mentioned above, which is required of all third-year doctoral students. The "best practice" exemplified here is research integrity training happening at different but appropriate stages of the student's career.

Similar pro-seminars are offered in the first year in Anthropology, Art and Archaeology, East Asian Studies, History, Ecology and Evolutionary Biology, Geosciences, Near Eastern Studies, and Psychology (Table I), while most of the language departments have pedagogy seminars that serve a similar purpose. In many cases these include professional topics like authorship, ethics, etc., thereby providing natural disciplinary venues for addressing many of the issues of scholarly integrity.

Another important factor is the close relationship between graduate education and research in most universities. Princeton took a significant step in that direction recently by creating the position of Dean for Research to complement that of the Dean of the Graduate School. This, together with the also new Keller Center for Innovation in Engineering Education in the School of Engineering and Applied Science, provides administrative capacity as well as commitment to advance on these issues. Furthermore, a sample of current graduate students were uniform in their appreciation of the existing courses, stating that more is needed and that a significant amount should be required. This reinforces our observations in several other professional development initiatives.

While the best practices cited above exist and are generally well received, only a small fraction of the graduate students participate and even that fraction only samples a portion of the offerings. This supports "The compelling need for a comprehensive approach to scholarly integrity" cited in the headline of the CGS *Communicator*.[1] The challenge is to

- propagate the existing best practices to reach a majority of the graduate students in the natural and social sciences and engineering,
- initiate other mechanisms to engage students from matriculation to graduation,
- differentiate the content appropriately for individual disciplines and the educational maturity of the students, and
- integrate it into all facets of graduate education, i.e. the departmental curriculum, teaching pedagogy, research groups and centers, and the operations of the Graduate School and Office of Research.

This is a large task that will require commitment and coordination across the campus, involving senior lecturers through the professorial faculty to the upper administration. Our sense is that such commitment exists in part already and may not be so difficult to nurture.

## TABLE I

**ANT 501 Proseminar in Anthropology:** A two-term survey of major anthropological writings, primarily for first-year graduate students. This seminar will focus on some major figures who have influenced anthropological theory and shaped our ideas of what anthropology is or should be. Historical formulations of some issues currently being revisited and hotly debated – e.g. rationalization and unreason, science and communication, subjectivity and dialogic encounters, and the status of knowledge and truth in the social sciences - will be examined.

**ART 500 Proseminar in the History of Art:** A course designed to inform students in the theoretical foundations of the discipline as well as in the methodological innovations of the last few decades. Required for incoming graduate students in the Western program. Students from other departments with methodological interests are also welcome.

**EAS 501, 502 Proseminar in Chinese and Japanese Studies:** General seminar dealing with the problems, methods, and possibilities of research peculiar to the fields of East Asian studies. Students may pursue their particular interests in their individual assignments, while participating in the general work of the seminar.

**HIS 500 Introduction to the Professional Study of History**: A colloquium to introduce the beginning graduate student to the great traditions in historical writing, a variety of techniques and analytical tools recently developed by historians, and the nature of history as a profession.

**EEB 505 Professional Topics**: The first part of this course focuses on grant-writing. First year students write a Sigma Xi (or similar-scale) grant application, while second year students start preparing a thesis proposal that could eventually become an NSF DDIG application. In some years a discussion of professional topics like authorship, ethics, etc. follows.

**GEO 505-506 Fundamentals of the Geosciences I:** A year-long survey of fundamental papers in the geosciences. Fall includes the origin and interior of the Earth, plate tectonics, geodynamics, the history of life on Earth, the composition of the Earth, its oceans and atmospheres, past climate. Spring includes present and future climate, biogeochemical processes in the ocean, geochemical cycles, orogenies, thermochronology, rock fracture and seismicity.

**NES 500 Introduction to the Professional Study of the Near East:** A departmental colloquium normally taken by all entering graduate students. It is designed to introduce students to reference and research tools, major trends in the scholarship of the field, and the faculty of the department.

**PSY 500/501/502 - Proseminar: Social/Cognitive/Neuroscience Psychology**. An intensive review, over the course of a full academic year, of several substantive areas of psychology, with an emphasis on the problems posed by the findings of contemporary research.

## References

1    CGS *Communicator*, Vol 41(3), June 2008. Available on website of the Council of Graduate Schools at http://www.cgsnet.org/portals/0/pdf/ comm_2008_06.pdf.

# Emerging Best Practices in Research and Scholarly Integrity: Preparing Students and Faculty of the Future for the New Ethical Demands

**Anthony G.O. Yeh**
**Dean of the Graduate School**
**The University of Hong Kong**

The University of Hong Kong has a *Policy for Ethical Practice in Research.* The Graduate School of the University of Hong Kong has been using the following methods to make sure that our students and teaching staff are aware of this policy and to prepare them to meet standards for research ethics:

## Students

1.  All new students are asked to sign a *Research Ethics Declaration Form* to declare that they have read and understood the university's *Policy for Ethical Practice in Research* so that they will be reminded that plagiarism and falsification of research data are serious academic misconduct.

2.  All new students are provided with the following circular and publications when they register:

    *   A circular from the Dean of Graduate School drawing students' attention to the existing rules and regulations against plagiarism and the serious consequences of an infringement ;

    *   University of Hong Kong's *Policy for Ethical Practice in Research,* which is also available on the Graduate School website (www.hku. hk/gradsch/web/student/ethics.htm);

    *   Booklet entitled *"What is Plagiarism?"* produced by the Registry, which is also available on the Graduate School website (www.hku. hk/plagiarism);

    *   Booklet entitled *"Plagiarism and How to Avoid It"* published by the Graduate School, which is also available on the Graduate School website (www.hku.hk/gradsch/web/resources);

- The *Graduate School Handbook,* which contains some sections on copyright and plagiarism. This is also available on the Graduate School website (www.hku.hk/gradsch/web/resources/handbooks/04/21.htm)

The Graduate School website also contains a section on Research Ethics under Information for Students (www.hku.hk/gradsch/web/student/ethics.htm).

3.  At the Orientation Programme and Induction Seminar conducted by the Graduate School each year, new students will be warned not to commit plagiarism and to comply with research ethics in carrying out their studies and research.

4.  The "Ethics & Research" course is offered as an elective module under the Graduate School Core Course II *Basic Research Skills and Methods.* This course offers a practical introduction, grounded in ethical theory, to moral questions research students are likely to confront. It introduces students to some of the ethical complexities and issues that challenge researchers today, and aims to enable students to deal sensitively with the moral challenges they will face in their research by introducing them to some of the related knowledge, skills and values. Starting from the next academic year, this module will be made compulsory so that all students will need to finish this course before doing their research.

5.  The Universitas 21 (U21) web module on "Global Research Ethics & Integrity" in which the Graduate School of the University of Hong Kong has participated and contributed to its development is now under testing and will be launched to our students when it is ready. This project was developed in the U21 Deans and Directors of Graduate Studies meeting in Vancouver in November 2005 and was followed up by a workshop in Hong Kong in November 2007. The project is managed by the University of Melbourne with a project advisory group composed of the Deans from Auckland, Edinburgh, Hong Kong, Melbourne and Nottingham.

6.  In the compulsory Graduate School Core Course "Introduction to Thesis Writing," students are reminded not to commit plagiarism and about the importance of research ethics. Since 2006, the teachers in the course have required all their students to submit their assignments to *Turnitin*

(www.turnitin.com) to check for plagiarism.

7. Email reminders under the subject "Reminder of Thesis Submission and Avoidance of Plagiarism" will be sent to students by the Graduate School six months before the end of their study period to remind them to complete a quality thesis in a timely manner. They are also reminded again that plagiarism and violation of research ethics is a serious academic misconduct and directed to references and guides on plagiarism and research ethics so as to help them avoid committing the offence.

8. The Graduate School has recently set up a mechanism on random checking of theses against plagiarism by using *Turnitin*. At the initial stage, a small percentage of the theses will be randomly picked by the Graduate School for submission to *Turnitin* before they can sit for the thesis examination. The student, supervisor and the Faculty Office concerned will be informed by the Graduate School when a student has been selected and the student will be required to submit a soft copy of his/her thesis to *Turnitin* and provide a copy of the *Turnitin* report to the supervisor for reading and judgement before examination.

## Teaching Staff

1. All new teaching staff members are made aware of the University's *Policy for Ethical Practice in Research*.

2. Research ethics is a component in a course on Postgraduate Supervision run by the Centre for the Advancement of University Teaching with input from the Graduate School.

3. Supervisors are constantly reminded of good practices for supervisors, which are available on the Graduate School web site www.hku.hk/gradsch/web/supervisor/good-super.htm. The web site also gives much emphasis to research ethics and safety.

# The Ethical and Psychological Implications of Research on Sensitive Topics

Professor Yvonne H. Carter
Dean, Warwick Medical School, and Pro-Vice-Chancellor
University of Warwick

## Introduction

As the public and legislators have become more aware of the sensitive nature of some research topics, UK universities have found themselves under further scrutiny regarding their research governance and ethics policies, procedures and frameworks. Recent legislation, such as the EC Clinical Trials Directive or the UK Human Tissue Act, the Mental Capacity Act, and changes in licensing of human embryo research have provoked universities to examine and, where necessary, improve and update their procedures and policies. The main research funders now require assurances at both the application and award stages that projects have, where necessary, been approved by an institution's ethics committee and that the research will be conducted within a research governance framework embedded within the institution. This increased focus on research governance within UK universities has been accompanied by development and reappraisal of ethical guidelines for researchers, particularly with regard to research on sensitive topics. For example, in 2006, the Economic and Social Research Council (ESRC) published guidance for all researchers submitting proposals for funding for social research projects.[1] This was partly in response to a growing awareness of the ethical issues arising in social research on sensitive topics.

## Research on Sensitive Topics at Warwick Medical School and across the University of Warwick

Biomedical research includes some of the most sensitive topics. At Warwick Medical School our clinical trials unit is involved in a range of research on sensitive topics including trials of cancer treatment in end stage disease, trials of interventions involving residents in nursing homes, and trials of emergency treatments in unconscious patients who cannot give consent. We also research on stem cells and our clinical researchers have studies in dementia, psychosis and depression, and a strong focus on ethnicity and mental health. Likewise biological science students are involved in animal research, and even plant biologists encounter sensitive research areas when studying gene modification.

However research on sensitive topics takes place across the university. Social Science PhD students are currently listing studies in such sensitive areas as disability, employment, children's rights, learning disability, adoption, reproductive health, migration, gender studies, old age, child safeguarding and adult protection, HIV transmission, health inequalities, and user involvement in health and social care. In the Institute of education, PhD students are studying sensitive areas of emotional development, such as inclusive education of disabled children, bullying and emotional abuse, and cross-cultural issues in education, and law students are researching criminality.

## Warwick's Approach to the Ethical and Psychological Implications of Research on Sensitive Topics

### Governance
At the University of Warwick, the University Research Ethics committee, (UREC,) established in 2003, is jointly chaired by two research Pro Vice-Chancellors, and has a very senior membership. The UREC provides the Council and the Senate with a detailed annual monitoring report on the operation of the research governance framework in the University and oversees a comprehensive ethical scrutiny process. The UREC and its sub-committees develop policies and guidance to facilitate the protection of the University's research participants.

### University Statement on the Ethical Conduct of Research
The University of Warwick is committed to advancing and safeguarding the highest academic and ethical standards in all its research activities. We are working closely with senior academics and administrative staff to ensure that all members of staff and students conducting and participating in research activity that involves participants, their data and/or tissue adopt the University's

- Research Code of Conduct,
- Code of Practice for Dealing with Allegations of Research Misconduct,
- Guidelines on Ethical Practice,
- Whistleblowing Code of Practice.

The University's ethics guidance for research students specifically emphasises the ethical implications of research on sensitive topics.[2] In addition to discussing research in situations where consent cannot be obtained, it states:

*3.5 In the case of non-invasive research methods such as interviews and questionnaires, the content and line of questioning may be highly sensitive, raise confidential, personal issues and intrude, or be perceived to intrude, upon a participant's comfort and privacy. The initial judgment on whether or not questions are sensitive and likely to cause harm rests with a lead researcher. For advice the lead researcher should consult the relevant University Research Ethics Sub-Committee.*

**Involvement of Patients and the Public**
The involvement of users (patients and the public) in the development of research can pre-empt problems in researching sensitive topics. At Warwick Medical School, all research students are advised and encouraged to involve patients and the public at all stages of the research, from developing the question through data collection and analysis to dissemination. Undergraduate medical students learn about user involvement in research in a Special Study Module in their clinical rotation. Warwick University hosts the National Health Service Centre for patient and public involvement. This Centre works closely with INVOLVE, a UK Government funded organization for developing user involvement in research. The University was one of the first to develop a standing user group for research (Warwick Diabetes Research User Group). The School of Health and Social studies hosts the Universities/User Teaching and Research Action Partnership (UNTRAP) which is a partnership between users of health and social care services, carers, and the Universities of Warwick and Coventry and the NHS.

**Conducting Specific Research on the Ethical Implications of Research on Sensitive Topics**
Senior researchers in our Clinical Trials Unit (CTU) have recognized the potential ethical difficulties of conducting research on sensitive topics, for example clinical trials on people with dementia and research on cardiac resuscitation. Several of the Unit's recent successful funding applications have included an ethicist as a co-applicant. The CTU is conducting research alongside some of these trials to look specifically at ethical issues of concern. For example a process evaluation of a trial of exercise therapy in residents of nursing homes is specifically looking at the consent process for residents

with mild to moderate cognitive impairment. A parallel sub study is exploring users' and carers' views of cluster randomized trials in vulnerable populations. The rationale for conducting this type of research alongside clinical trials, and the methodology required for such research, will form part of our new doctoral training programme in biomedical research.

## Supporting and Nurturing Researchers

Research on sensitive topics also has ethical and psychological implications for the researchers. Students and junior researchers are particularly vulnerable to the adverse psychological effects of this kind of research as they may not have the skills or experience to recognize and respond to problems as they arise. Warwick Medical School provides support for research students on a number of levels.

## Supervision

Supervisors have some of the most important roles in supporting doctoral students. Amongst their other responsibilities, Supervisors are expected: *To advise students on matters of confidentiality or ethical considerations relating to particular techniques, sources, or results.*

Within the Medical School, our Director of Research Degrees is supported by deputies in each research institute. Each maintains regular contact with students, and the Staff Student Liaison Committee (SSLC) affords opportunities for students to contribute to improved processes. A senior member of the academic staff of the medical school acts as an independent advisor to research students. Upgrade from MPhil to PhD registration occurs when a student has completed a full review and been assessed by an upgrade panel, which explores the ethical and psychological dimensions of sensitive research in addition to scientific considerations.

## Personal Development

The University of Warwick Professional and Research Development (PRD) is designed for postgraduate researchers and aims to help them plan a programme of research training suited to their particular needs and to serve as a record of the skills acquired during research at Warwick. It is based on the Research Councils' list of competencies that postgraduate researchers are expected to have or develop during their research, including the need to demonstrate awareness of issues relating to the rights of other researchers, of research subjects, and of others who may be affected by the research.

## Communities of Practice

Warwick Medical School works hard to develop local junior research communities, with shared facilities and regular research student seminars in each of our institutes, and to involve research students in the activities of the wider university and beyond. In the later stages of doctoral studies research students are encouraged to avail themselves of the 'time out' afforded by the UK GRAD Programme to attend a 3-5 day GRADschool, facilitating guided reflection in a safe space with peers.

### Taught Components of Research Training

Our emphasis on research training is moving towards **doctoral schools**, where the taught components are designed for integration with research development. These schools demonstrate to funding councils a comprehensive development programme for early researchers. The first of these at Warwick was the cross-disciplinary Doctoral School in Complexity Science, and we now have an MRC Doctoral School in Biomedical Science. There is still a place for component courses and WMS offers an MSc in Research Methods in Health Sciences as well as standalone modules on Clinical Research Governance.

### Values-Based Practice: Towards a More Supportive Framework for Research Scientists

Work at Warwick Medical School on the Philosophy of Mental Health has led to the development of 'Values-based Practice' (VBP) which is the subject of ongoing research, following its uptake into Mental Health Practice. Essentially VBP equips clinicians or researchers with tools to identify the values at play in any given situation. Making reference to ethical frameworks, VBP is intended to support decision making (alongside evidence-based practice) in situations of complexity or where values conflict. A current research objective of WMS is to implement and evaluate this approach within research development and practice, using our Clinical Trials Unit as a pilot.

## References

1   Economic and Social Research Council. Research Ethics Framework. ESRC (2005). Accessed 06.08.08 from http://www.esrc.ac.uk/ESRCInfo Centre/Images/ESRC_Re_Ethics_Frame_tcm6-11291.pdf.

2   Guidelines on Ethical Practice, University of Warwick. Accessed 06.08.08 from http://www2.warwick.ac.uk/services/rss/services/ethics/statement/guidance/ethicsguidance.pdf.

# The Ethical and Psychological Implications of Research on Sensitive Topics

Robyn Owens
Pro-Vice Chancellor of Research and Research Training
The University of Western Australia

Risk minimization and management have become standard practices across many sectors of employment, from the professions to blue-collar fields. Surgeons wear masks and gloves so as not to infect or be infected by patients; fighter pilots have ejector seats; chemists, bee keepers and construction workers are amongst those who safeguard themselves from hazardous materials by wearing protective clothing, and there are specialised training programmes to support therapists who work with trauma survivors [1, 2]. Debriefings are commonly available to such specialists, as are preventative strategies such as peer support programs, good supervisory support, stress management, self-awareness of vulnerabilities, and worker self-care plans at induction. The term *vicarious traumatisation* was first used by McCann & Pearlman [3], who developed a framework for understanding the psychological effects of empathic exposure to individuals' trauma experiences (see also [4]). Indeed, mechanisms to prevent vicarious traumatisation, defined as "… the impact on the therapist of repeated exposure to traumatic client imagery and material" [5], are being implemented across the mental health professions. Yet, even though trauma studies have emerged as an area of interdisciplinary research over the past two decades, scholars of potentially traumatic research topics are not protected from the potential adverse effects of the material they study.

Vicarious traumatisation is widely recognised as an inevitable occupational hazard for mental health professionals working with severely traumatised people. It is likely that the same will be true for scholars of natural, technological and human-induced catastrophes. Perhaps more so, as it is the nature of academic life that one's research topic is all-embracing: academics do not have nine-to-five jobs; they tend to live their research without boundaries. How do those researching traumatic events – from family violence, sexual abuse, and suicide to life-threatening illnesses and tsunamis, warfare involving children, terrorism, genocide and refugee issues – cope with their disturbing subject matter? Does their research – whether it is exposure to literature, oral testimony, artefacts or archival material – affect their lives and if so, in what ways? Does their research topic have a cumulative transformative effect on their identity, worldview, life choices and relationships? Are they left suffering lasting emotional and psychological consequences or do they separate their daily lives from their research, and if so, how is this achieved?

It is difficult to accurately assess the extent to which scholars are exposed to potentially traumatic material but we sampled the research topics of current and past research projects at The University of Western Australia, revealing projects ranging from child sexual abuse, spousal homicide, familicide, work on the Stolen Generations, memories of the Armenian genocide, teacher strategies for self-harming school children, and studies of miscarriage and stillbirth. In the discipline of Social Work & Social Policy alone there are currently 15 PhD students researching topics that have the potential to traumatise. The Medical Faculty has research students studying palliative care, depression, suicide, or substance abuse, and students in the Centre for Forensic Science research the effects of drugs on road safety or the relationship between child sexual abuse and adult psychopathology. All such PhD students, as research trainees, are vulnerable to the potentially traumatising impacts of their work. Yet, universities do not have formal mechanisms to identify and prepare scholars for the potentially traumatic effects that may result from the material they study.

Of course, it is not inevitable that all researchers of traumatic topics will suffer adverse effects from the material they study. According to McCann & Pearlman [3] and Pearlman and Saakvitne [6], aspects of the work and characteristics intrinsic to the individual such as personality, personal history, current personal circumstances and professional development interact to produce unique effects of vicarious traumatisation (see also [7]). Pearlman and Mac Ian [8] found that counselors with a history of personal trauma showed greater disruptions to their cognitive schemata than those without such a history. It is not uncommon for academics to be drawn to research topics that are close to the heart and which may help them make sense of their past or present personal circumstances. Pearlman and Mac Ian also found that the level of experience can influence vicarious traumatisation, with newer therapists experiencing the most difficulties. It is plausible that scholars researching potentially traumatic events will be particularly vulnerable to vicarious traumatisation when they are new to research (as are most PhD students) and when their own personal histories intersect with their research topics.

As we well know, research students face a variety of potential stressors during candidature. In order to help them overcome these barriers and concurrently to retain students and hasten completion rates, most universities provide a range of support, including advice about navigating relations with supervisors, assistance with negotiating a work-life balance and strategies for tackling procrastination and self-sabotage. But do we prepare students for potential stresses related to the nature of the topic being researched?

Pilot research being undertaken at The University of Western Australia aims to identify PhD students who may be vulnerable to distress and/or trauma due to their field of study. A survey instrument has been designed which analyses responses of PhD students to a range of questions in three main categories. One set of questions is concerned with identifying research topics that are identified as potentially traumatic (have you experienced stress or anxiety related to your research topic?). The other sets of questions are concerned with the characteristics of the PhD student (including predisposition to stress and anxiety), the student experience (including but not limited to supervisor satisfaction, feelings of belonging to a research community, available resources), and external influences (such as whether the student has a scholarship, hours of paid employment, and family responsibilities).

Responses will be analyzed by structural equation modeling, using Lisrel. We aim to identify factors likely to contribute to the distress or trauma of PhD students who have self-identified as working on projects that are associated directly or indirectly with the study of suffering. Once PhD students who are potentially vulnerable to distress or trauma are identified, preventative strategies can be implemented.

I have raised this as an issue for the Strategic Leaders Summit on Graduate Education and Research Ethics, as I believe that it is important that we start addressing these questions, for the benefit of individual researchers, universities, and society more broadly. From a narrow economic-efficiency perspective, implementation of additional support for students studying potentially traumatic topics should impact positively on completion times and retention rates. Universities need to act without delay because failure to identify and provide ways for researchers to work through vicarious trauma could have detrimental effects on the mental health and well being of their employees and research students. Indeed, it would be prudent for universities to confront these questions before they find themselves facing demands for compensation from researchers – staff or PhD students – based on claims that they have neglected their duty of care. The potential for legal recourse would be best avoided. From a broader perspective, failure to identify and provide ways for researchers to work through trauma could not only have detrimental effects on their mental health but could also jeopardise the study of catastrophic events and in turn the lessons we learn from them, which can have implications for the future of humankind.

**Acknowledgements:** This research is being undertaken in collaboration with Judith Berman, Loretta Ho, Colin MacLeod and David Morrison and is funded by the Graduate Research School at The University of Western Australia.

## References:

1.  Kathleen Kendall-Tackett. (2003). Clinical self-care when working with adult survivors. In *Treating the Lifetime Health Effects of Childhood Victimization: A Guide for Mental Health, Medical and Social Service Professionals*, New York: Civic Research Institute.

2.  Vicarious Traumatisation, Occupational Health and Safety Draft Policy (no date), Women's Health Statewide, Government of South Australia. Accessed 27 July 2008 from http://www.whs.sa.gov.au/pub/draft_VT_polic_1.pdf.

3.  I. L McCann, & L. A. Pearlman. (1990). Vicarious traumatization: A framework for understanding the psychological effects of working with victims. *Journal of Traumatic Stress*, vol. 3, no. 1, 131-151.

4.  C. R. Figley, (Ed.). (1995). *Compassion Fatigue: Coping with Secondary Traumatic Stress Disorder in Those who Treat the Traumatized*. New York: Brunner/Mazel.

5.  Lyndall Steed & Robyn Downing. (1998). A phenomenological study of vicarious traumatisation amongst psychologists and professional counsellors working in the field of sexual abuse/assault. *The Australasian Journal of Disaster and Trauma Studies*, vol. 2. Accessed 27 July 2008 from http://www.massey.ac.nz/~trauma/issues/1998-2/steed.htm.

6.  L. A. Pearlman & K.W. Saakvitne. (1995). Treating therapists with vicarious traumatisation and secondary traumatic stress disorders, in C. R. Figley, (Ed). *Compassion Fatigue: Coping with Secondary Traumatic Stress Disorder in Those who Treat the Traumatized*. New York: Brunner/ Mazel, 150-178.

7.  J. Dunkley & T. A. Whelan. (Feb. 2006). Vicarious traumatisation: current status and future directions. *British Journal of Guidance & Counselling*, vol. 34, no. 1.

8.  L. A. Pearlman & P. S. Mac Ian. (1995). Vicarious traumatisation: An empirical study of the effects of trauma work on trauma therapists.

*Professional Psychology, Research and Practice*, 26:66, 558-565, American Psychological Association; cited in L. Sexton. Vicarious traumatisation of counsellors and effects on their workplaces. (1999). *British Journal of Guidance and Counselling*, vol. 27, Issue 3.

# V. WHAT ARE THE GLOBAL ISSUES SHAPING EDUCATION AND TRAINING IN RESEARCH?

## Summary of Presentations and Group Discussion:

The fifth session of the Global Leaders Summit examined the global forces that are currently reshaping graduate research communities. The purpose of this session was to better understand two particular shifts in global research environments and the implications of these shifts for issues of scholarly integrity: first, the increase in international collaborations in the areas of research and education, a change that increases the mobility of students and researchers and creates new international communities of research; and second, the reorganization of processes of publication and data management, especially through the emergence of new technologies for producing and disseminating knowledge. Both of these transitions create new research cultures, some local to a place, some "virtual." As many of the summit participants observed, however, graduate communities have not yet created structures to understand these new environments and to ensure that they operate with clear ethical standards. Participants also agreed that work must be done to help graduate students and faculty respond to the ethical problems raised by these new research environments. **Daniel Denecke**, Director of Best Practices at the Council of Graduate Schools, emphasized these concerns in his presentation for this session, stating that graduate schools are still working to catch up to these significant global changes.

In the first part of the session, on **cultural aspects of international research and educational collaboration,** participants discussed various tools used by their institutions to make ethical standards more transparent and to build a foundation for creating shared standards. While comparing ethics standards with international partners is often perceived to be an activity that supports collaboration, participants noted that it can have the additional benefit of clarifying domestic frameworks already in place. For example, one participant observed that international research collaborations had provided her university with the incentive to accelerate their own process of self-assessment so that they could compare standards with a foreign partner. **Xiao-ling Liao** of Peking University added to this point when she explained that the internationalization of graduate education had prompted Chinese universities to meet competitive international standards, although she also noted that it is important to protect graduate research and education from the negative influences of global competition. Throughout this discussion, it was agreed that codes and other regulatory frameworks are most valuable when they serve to educate researchers about ethical standards (not merely punish those who violate them). For example, **Isaac Mazonde** of the University of Botswana noted that the Internal Review Board created at his university had led researchers to reflect more carefully about the ethical dimensions of their projects and raise the ethical standards of their work.

In the second part of the session, participants discussed the difficult ethical questions raised by **new technologies for managing data and publishing research**. **Maxwell King**'s paper focused on the increasing interest among Australian graduate students in the electronic publication of dissertations, a trend that has raised questions about how strictly this form of publication should be constrained by copyright laws. **Clark Hulse** of the University of Illinois at Chicago observed that the trend of internet publication is one that students and faculty find difficult to navigate because it carries contradictory messages—a push toward "open access" to scholarship in the public domain on the one hand, an insistence on authorial rights on the other. It was agreed that widened access to scholarship requires a more complex system of coordination between the various individuals and bodies involved in the publication process. Participants also expressed a need for more information about the wide variety of issues within this larger topic— for example, clearer language to define concepts like "free use" and authorship. Comparing different institutional definitions of these terms is an important part of the process of responding to, and shaping, these new online communities of research and publication.

# Intercultural Differences and Scholarly Integrity in Graduate International Collaborations

### Daniel D. Denecke
### Director, Best Practices
### Council of Graduate Schools

Prior conferences and international forums have focused on policy coordination among predominantly national bodies responsible for investigating research misconduct and "policing" the research community.[1] Topics discussed in this arena have included: regulatory issues, compliance, and the desirability of harmonizing terminology, standards, investigation procedures and "deterrence" mechanisms. This broad policy context is an important one, and the greater coordination of national policies will be helpful for addressing compliance issues that researchers face when they pursue international collaborations. Also important will be any resources that may emerge from these discussions that promote greater understanding about core questions such as: How do policies differ by country? Who is responsible for investigating misconduct in each country and/or institution? and, How are national policy differences adjudicated when problems arise?

But all research and educational collaborations take place in institutional contexts, and in these contexts what we call cultural factors are potentially of equal if not greater importance than the regulatory policies in shaping decisions, behaviors, attitudes and expectations of students and faculty. Since 2004, the Council of Graduate Schools has worked with 18 universities across two national projects in the U.S. to advance the responsible conduct of research. An original contract from the U.S. Office of Research Integrity (2004-06) and a subsequent grant from the National Science Foundation (2006-08) have made possible CGS sponsorship of pilot projects that address those cultural factors that pertain to graduate education and training in the responsible conduct of research (RCR).[2] CGS has embarked on a new multi-year initiative, the Project for Scholarly Integrity, and over the next several years will work closely with a network of five universities to develop models for a comprehensive approach to scholarly integrity in graduate education.[3] These projects will include traditional RCR areas (such as human subjects research, data management, and authorship issues) as well as a wider range of activities and issues that cut across disciplines and scholarly responsibilities (such as classroom practice and financial stewardship). Across these projects,

CGS member deans have demonstrated that strategic leaders on campus can be instrumental in promoting the development and sharing of innovative resources and practices that can bring about change in the institution. While international collaboration was not a specific focus of these projects, the graduate deans who led them frequently observed in group discussion that intercultural and international differences are important areas where further progress needs to be made.[4]

Discussions of research integrity in the context of international collaboration inevitably touch on the "cultural issues" that may arise and the need for greater intercultural understanding for those collaborations to succeed. Such discussions imply that nations and regions each have potentially unique systems of meanings, values, orientations, techniques, and behaviors that can shape or influence scholars' decision-making and research behavior. At best, the assumption that a student's nationality requires cultural sensitivities on the part of graduate programs and institutions can result in improved understanding of the differences in learning styles and the enhanced preparation of young scholars. When such sensitivities are poorly expressed or inadequately structured, however, such thinking can reinforce stereotypes and result in inconsistencies in expectations or procedures or in programming that targets certain subpopulations of students where a broader student population could potentially benefit. In the educational context, our vocabulary for addressing the cultural differences that may arise in international educational collaborations is still underdeveloped. Empirical studies and innovative educational programs will likely be important as international collaborations at the graduate level (including joint and dual degree programs, student and faculty exchange programs, and research collaborations) become ever more common.

But there are other cultural differences that intersect with issues of research ethics and scholarly integrity in graduate education and research. Even in a graduate program comprised only of one country's domestic faculty and students, there may be generational, ethnic, and (in interdisciplinary programs, especially) disciplinary differences that could all pose potential challenges to traditional educational approaches to scholarly integrity. And as one graduate dean on the planning committee for the CGS Project for Scholarly Integrity observed, undergraduates in the U.S. also could be said to have their own research culture, which must be understood in order to best shape the orientation and early transitional year(s) of a graduate program. Compound these "cultural" differences with the complex array of differences involved in any international collaboration and one can appreciate the complexity of intercultural issues that may arise in devising graduate education programs devoted to issues of research integrity.

Beyond the educational setting, where cultural issues involving international students may need to be carefully addressed, there are the research and institutional settings, where cultural issues may arise that can threaten the success of international collaborations and compromise the commitments of both administrators and researchers to scholarly integrity. In the research setting, there are nine core topics traditionally covered in RCR training: [1) acquisition, management, sharing, and ownership of data; 2) conflict of interest and commitment; 3) human subjects; 4) animal welfare; 5) research misconduct (falsification, fabrication, plagiarism); 6) publication practices and responsible authorship; 7) mentor/trainee responsibilities; 8) peer review; and 9) collaborative science.[5]] Each of these arguably has international and intercultural dimensions. For example, in the area of data management, sharing and ownership, a typical problem that may arise concerns cases in which international research partners have not articulated a memorandum of understanding in advance about which institution will own the data at the project's conclusion or in the event that the collaboration falls apart.[6] In the area of human subjects research, some populations (such as Native American tribes in the U.S.) may have autonomous political sovereignty and their own ethics review boards and processes for approving the collection and publication of human subjects research,[7] and governments may have advisories and foreign policies concerning specific countries that can impact human subjects research and international collaborations and student exchanges in ways that sometimes pose problems only when the proposed collaborations reach the final stages of administrative approval.

A key cultural difference that CGS projects in research and scholarly integrity have addressed includes that between faculty and administration. Although both groups are committed to excellence in education and research, nearly every faculty member and graduate dean will confirm that there are times when it seems as though faculty and senior administrators speak different languages, cherish different values, and could therefore be said to inhabit different cultures.[8] Researchers encounter obstacles and barriers in international collaborations when scholarly integrity is compromised by inadequate information about comparative institutional and national policies and practices for promoting integrity. One of the key issues upon which international discussions of the kind this 2008 Strategic Leaders Global Summit on Graduate Education in Research Ethics and Scholarly Integrity could help to address is the need for greater "intercultural dialogue" around the world between researchers and strategic leaders. Facing these barriers and overcoming obstacles has typically been a matter for each pair of institutions involved in an international collaboration to achieve on its own. Thus, even when institutions build on the prior intercultural understanding fostered by pre-existing relationships, international collaborations often require institutions to reinvent the wheel of policy coordination with every new challenge.[9] When this is not possible, and international differences prove insurmountable because they have not been understood and discussed in the planning stages, serious incidents of misconduct and important research and educational opportunities can fall through the cracks.

There is evidence that institutions are developing and planning increasing numbers of formal and informal international research and educational collaborations at the graduate level, which could have tremendous implications for the exchange of ideas, faculty/researchers, and students. If these collaborations succeed, we may well be witnessing the emergence of a new geography for advanced scholarship as important as the creation of the ancient Silk Road trade routes connecting the East and the West or the great Venetian and Genoese trade routes of the 13th and 14th centuries that revolutionized the Mediterranean. The identifying of mechanisms for promoting greater intercultural understanding and information exchange between faculty and strategic leaders—on an institutional, a national, and an international scale—would be one very direct and tangible approach, with potential benefits to all, for addressing the complex intercultural issues that arise in international collaborations.

## References

1    Such important forums would include, for example, the 2007 Lisbon Conference supported by the European Commission and organized by the European Science Foundation and the Office of Research Integrity (http://www.esf.org/activities/esf-conferences/details/2007/confdetail242.html) as well as the OECD Global Science Forum (see "Best Practices for Ensuring Scientific Integrity and Preventing Misconduct," (http://www.oecd.org/dataoecd/37/17/40188303.pdf).

2    Two publications that resulted from these initiatives include *Graduate Education for the Responsible Conduct of Research* (CGS, 2007) and *Best Practices in Graduate Education for the Responsible Conduct of Research* (CGS, 2008 in press).

3    See CGS June 2008 *Communicator*: "The Compelling Need for a Comprehensive Approach to Scholarly Integrity." For additional project information and project updates, see also the CGS web site: www.cgsnet. org ("Programs" > "Responsible Conduct of Research Initiatives").

4    See "The Compelling Need" (CGS June 2008 *Communicator*).

5    Nicholas Steneck, *Introduction to the Responsible Conduct of Research*. (2004). Washington, DC: U.S. Government Printing Office, p. ix.

6    On the causes for breakdowns in international collaborations, see Heidi Ledford, (2008,) With All Good Intentions, *Nature, 452(10)*, 682-684.

7    See Daniel Vasgird. (2007). Making Research Trustworthy for Native Americans. *Journal of Empirical Research on Human Research Ethics* 2(1), 84-5.

8    See Ledford, With All Good Intentions and Christine Boesz and Nigel Lloyd, (2008,) Investigating International Misconduct, *Nature, 452(10)*, 686-687.

9    See the Council of Graduate Schools, *Global Perspectives on Graduate Education: Proceedings of the Strategic Leaders Global Summit on Graduate Education* (CGS, 2008).

# Some Deliberation on the Internationalization of Chinese Postgraduate Education

Xiao-ling Liao

Director of Association of Chinese Graduate Schools (ACGS)

Graduate School of Peking University, Beijing, China

Accompanying economic globalization, the internationalization of postgraduate education has become a topic of significant focus. In this revolutionary yet delicate atmosphere, the question of how best to approach the inevitable internationalization of Chinese postgraduate education has become the major point of interest for educators in China.

## I. Internationalization and Localization of Postgraduate Education

Postgraduate education is a highly important component of higher education; it is conducted to produce elite scholars and scientists who shoulder the vital task of responding to scientific problems of great national value. The quality of a nation's postgraduate education is a direct reflection of its overall national strength and creative capability. With the strong tide of internationalization in higher education, the internationalization of postgraduate education is expected without a doubt.

The purpose of internationalizing postgraduate education is to have the educational policies, strategies, and the quality of graduates match the international standard and for degrees and diplomas granted to be recognized on an international scale. This issue includes topics such as curriculum, student backgrounds, mentoring, internship activities, educational theory, educational mode, certification and assessment, etc.

Concerning postgraduate education, internationalization and localization are two effects of the same issue. Internationalization promotes universal values with the characteristics of the modern age; localization has more particularity and takes a different form within each individual nation. Postgraduate education has had a late start in China, and even though we have experienced tremendous growth in the past years there is still an undeniable distance between us and the more developed countries. Whilst adopting a tolerant, understanding attitude towards the predominance of more developed postgraduate educations, we have also taken daring steps to merge into the mainstream, and we are achieving rapid development by participating in international competition.

This situation is also beneficial to the development of Chinese postgraduate education itself.

At the same time, blossoming from 5000 years of civilization, Chinese postgraduate education has strong roots and characteristics of its own. In the past 30 years, we have granted approximately 130,000 doctorate degrees and over a million master's degrees. We have also contributed greatly to the preservation, development and promotion of Chinese culture worldwide. Experiences have proven: When learning from foreign higher educational systems, if internationalization and localization are balanced well, higher education can become a powerful ally to the growth of society. By observing the methods and theories adopted by developed countries, we have made continuous adjustments to update our postgraduate education and build the pro-research university model. Currently, the government has given heavy funds to universities working on research programs such as "project 985" and "project 211." The government has also approved of the establishment of 56 independent "graduate schools." We focus on producing highly educated personnel aimed to meet the practical requirements of modern Chinese society; we have formed the major outlines of a unique system of education, in theory and in practice. The favored solution adopted by us is to emphasize both the internationalization and the localization of Chinese postgraduate education. We are confident that with more practical experiences and flexible and creative policies, Chinese postgraduate education will mature and perfect with due time.

## II. Concerning Research Ethics in the Internationalization of Chinese Postgraduate Education

Concerning attitude, we must understand the importance of connecting our education to the mainstream of the world. Concerning policies, we need to establish open and flexible policies so as to meet rapid changes whilst creating a reputable and legalized atmosphere. Concerning practices, we must bear in mind cultural differences and respect individuality whilst striving towards internationalization. Concerning academics, we must create research teams of international standards for scientific research and mentoring, searching for a new method of education that has an internationalized system of courses and degrees and creating international collaboration in educational and academic fields. Concerning development, we need to adapt to the changes the new age brings; we also need to be remain vigilant about ethical problems in research, learn from experiences of developed countries, and make adjustments to meet the requirements of the new era.

Whilst promoting the internationalization of Chinese postgraduate education, we especially take care to prevent problems of research ethics. The already existing ethical problems belonging to each individual country may combine and enlarge in the atmosphere of economic globalization. For example: Due to the different level of education and research status of each country, as well as the language differences, there are people who have found "loop-holes," a possibility to simply take existing results of others as their own. (Mostly this occurs when researchers translate the works of a foreign language, or abstract results from them.)

Another example: Due to the different evaluation systems of each country, and the different evaluation standards, there are people who are willing to exaggerate the quality of their works and their research abilities to achieve a winning situation when competing for funding or other resources on an international scale. More specifically, in Peking University and Nanjing University, there has been a highly publicized expulsion of two professors due to serious research ethical issues, of which they were found guilty beyond a reasonable doubt.

From all the examples given above, it is more than obvious that in China, our government and university officials have a strict approach toward problems of research ethics; unethical scholars will not be tolerated under any circumstances.

A reputable educational aura will attract educators and students alike; in addition, the quality of graduates will be more reliable. The Chinese government believes research ethics to be highly important, and we have actively promoted laws and regulations concerning international collaboration to create a clear and legal atmosphere for both domestic and foreign educators. Regulations have been established such as "Regulations for Chinese-Foreign compatible degree," "Practice Regulations" and "Regulations concerning over-sea branches of Chinese universities." At the same time, most of our universities have established policies of their own concerning this matter, such as: "Specifications on research ethics for scholars" of Peking University, "Specification on research ethics for postgraduate students" of University of Science and Technology of China, etc. We have confidence that with all the methods above and adjustments we may make in due time, the internationalization of Chinese postgraduate education will grow in a healthy environment.

Research ethics issues exist in every country and the situation in China is no exception. Despite all this we believe that as the conscience and awareness of scholars grow, as laws and regulations mature in due time, working alongside colleagues from all over the world, the internationalization of Chinese postgraduate education has a bright and promising future ahead.

Special thanks to Principle Qifeng Zhou, for his guidance. Special thanks to Lei Guo and Feng He of Graduate school of Peking University, for their contribution to the statistics concerned in this paper.

## References:

China Scholarship Council, official website, http://www.csc.edu.cn.

Chen Xue-fei (1997). Internationalization of Higher Education: Perspectives from History, Theory to Strategy. "Shanghai Research in Higher Education" (11).

Clark, Burton R. (2001). A Place of Inquiry: Research and Advanced Education in Modern Universities. Hang-zhou Education Press.

"Degree and Postgraduate Education Development Program" (2006-2020) (2007).

Liu Dao-yu, The Strategic Choice of Chinese Higher Education Internationalization. "Higher Education Research" (4).

Ministry of Education of the People's Republic of China, official website, http://www.moe.gov.cn.

Wang Xu-hui, Motivations and Patterns of Internationalization of Higher Education (2007). "Liaoning Education Research" (8).

Xu Ke-yi (2006). Discussion on Internationalization and Localization of Graduate Education. "Academic Degrees & Graduate Education" (2).

Yang Fu-jia (2001). Internationalization: the Inevitable Trend of Higher Education Development. "Higher Education in China"(3).

# Responsible Conduct of Research at the University of Botswana

Isaac Mazonde
Director of Research
University of Botswana

## I.  Background to Ethics Legislation in Botswana

In Botswana, there is no ethics legislation other than the anthropological act of 1971, which was created to protect Bushmen studied in research projects. This legislation has caused problems because it has not adequately addressed more recent issues that have emerged—for example, in South Africa's use of blood samples taken in Botswana.  Blood samples are moved from Botswana to South Africa (a country that provides Botswana with medical services), without any ethical consideration; the ownership of specimens and disposal rights need to be more clearly defined.  There is no equivalent to the Office of Research Integrity in Botswana to oversee such matters.

## II.  Introduction to Ethical Standards at the University

In spite of a lack of ethics legislation in the country as a whole, the University of Botswana is committed to promoting an intellectual environment that stimulates scholarly work and the responsible conduct of research.  The university expects all members of the UB community to maintain high ethical standards in research.  Academic staff are responsible for the integrity of all research carried out under their supervision, regardless of who actually performs the work. Students are responsible for adhering to the principles that underlie the responsible conduct of research at all times.  The university further expects all researchers to adhere to internationally accepted research standards in their various disciplines.  The term "all researchers" applies to all persons affiliated with UB, including academic, support, and technical staff; students and trainees; visiting academics and collaborators.

Any allegation of research misconduct should be delivered to a university official.

For academic staff that official may be: a Dean, Deputy Vice Chancellor,

Vice Chancellor, or the Chairperson of the Research Risks Committee. The procedure for investigating an allegation of research misconduct is available from the office of Research and Development.

For students that official may be: a Dean, or a member of the academic staff. The procedure for investigating an allegation of research misconduct is described in the student Academic Honesty Policy.

Variations from the normal procedures may occur when unusual circumstances so warrant. Every reasonable effort will be made to process an allegation expediently.

## III.   Areas of Focused Attention

The University of Botswana has hired an Assistant Director for Ethics who is responsible for all aspects of research ethics at the university. The university has also mounted RCR seminars to address issues of scholarly integrity that are deemed to be especially important. These include: the management of research funds, conflict of interest and conflict of commitment, data management, authorship, and the protection of whistle-blowers. Information on developments in some of these areas is outlined below.

**Procedures for Reporting Research Misconduct**
It is the responsibility of every person associated the UB to report observed or suspected instances of research misconduct. A person who is unsure as to whether an incident falls within the definition of research misconduct, may discuss his/her concern confidentially and informally with the Chairperson of the Research Risks Committee (RRC) before deciding whether to file a formal allegation of misconduct. Contact details for the RRC Chairman are available from the Office of Research and Development (ORD). Data suggest that many suspected cases of research misconduct arise due to misunderstandings. Therefore, the Complainant is encouraged to seek resolution to the problem within the department or Faculty before filing a formal complaint.

**Retaliation**
Protection of the "whistle-blower," the person who, in good faith, files an allegation of research misconduct concerning another member of the UB community, is critical to successful adherence to the principles of research ethics.

Normally an allegation of research misconduct will not be acted upon if it is submitted anonymously. This is because the process of investigation cannot be carried out effectively if only the Respondent is available to be interviewed. However, the Complaintant can ask that his/her name be withheld when the Respondent is asked to respond to the allegation. In such a case, every reasonable effort will be taken to maintain the confidentiality of the name of the Complaintant.

UB is committed to ensuring the protection of the "whistle-blower" from any form of university discrimination as a result of submitting a good-faith allegation of research misconduct. All allegations, inquiries, investigations and reports about possible research misconduct are considered confidential. Divulging confidential information is a breach of trust and constitutes misconduct. Any person who submits a good-faith allegation of research misconduct, or who provides information during an inquiry or investigation, shall be free from restraint, coercion, or reprisal by UB for his/her participation in this process.

## Retention and Ownership of Data

Researchers should pay careful attention to the procedures they employ in collecting and recording data. Ideally, research data should be entered in ink in a bound notebook that has numbered pages, and the researcher should date and sign the entries at the end of each day. Not only does this provide an accurate record of the research, but it also can assist the researcher to recall at a later date observations that may have seemed unimportant earlier. This is an important protection if questions arise later about priority in making an important observation, or when there is possibility of a patent from the research.

Attention also should be given to the storage of data. Research data should be kept in a secure location. Most researchers retain their original data and their computerized data analysis permanently, because as a field develops, that data may shed light on a question that arises many years later. The stored data should be sufficiently complete so that it can be used to reconstruct the study if there is a question about the validity of the conclusions.

When the research is funded by an extramural agency, the research data belong to that agency. It is important that ownership be understood by all parties before the project is started. In most cases a non-profit funding agency will give the intellectual property rights and rights to the data to the researcher. However, for-profit companies may have restrictive policies that limit the rights of the researcher to long-term access to the data.

When the research is funded by UB or carried out by UB staff, UB has the rights to the data. However, normally the university is not interested in keeping research data, and therefore will cede the rights to the researcher. The ownership policy is required because the university is legally responsible for all professional activities carried out by its employees and students.

**The Internal Review Board**

Before the University of Botswana had an IRB, there was a sub-committee for funding that was used to administer the university's funding resources. After the IRB was created, we made sure that all cases that had been approved for funding would be taken to the IRB for approval. The IRB seems to have had a very positive effect: we have found that project proposals significantly improved between the first and second rounds of evaluation. The majority of applications that did not pass on the first round were able to pass on the second.

# *Authorship and Plagiarism in the Global Era*

**Clark Hulse**
**Associate Chancellor and Dean of the Graduate College**
**University of Illinois at Chicago**

I want to start with three changes regarding electronic publication at my institution, none of which is unique, and which therefore may illustrate significant issues about authorship, authorial rights, and plagiarism.

Recently the Committee on Institutional Cooperation—of which my university is a part—entered into a broad agreement to digitize up to 10 million volumes, out of 75 million total volumes, as part of the Google Book Search project. Other universities across the globe have also joined this project. Out of it will emerge a massive shared digital repository of public domain holdings.

On one hand, this project is a huge step forward toward a fundamental value not only of science but of all intellectual inquiry—widely-shared, open and near-instantaneous access to knowledge. At the same time, it creates fundamental challenges to our notions of authorship and intellectual property, notions that lie at the center of the systems of values that constitute academic integrity or academic misconduct.

The Google Book Search project includes vast amounts of material that is still under copyright. Its digital archive creates the potential for eventual licensing agreements for this material that would broaden access even further. At the same time, copyright holders have challenged the Google archive and search technology—which makes available excerpts from works in copyright—on the grounds that it will allow texts to be disintegrated into word-strings, disseminated, and reassembled at will outside of copyright. Paradoxically, that same ability to search word-strings has made it much easier to detect plagiarism and hence to reassert intellectual ownership including copyright.

The second change has occurred in parallel with the Google Book Search project, as the CIC provosts have adopted and recommended to their faculties a standard Addendum to Publication Agreements. Through it, a faculty member, as a condition of assigning copyright to a publisher, asserts:

- the author's own non-exclusive rights to the work,
- the non-exclusive right of the author and author's employer to make the work available over the internet 6 months after its publication, and
- the non-exclusive right of the author's employer to use the work in

teaching and research within the institution.

Together these policies mark a reassertion of the authorial rights of both the individual researcher and the university in distinction from those of journal and book publishers. At the same time, they attempt to reassert the importance and scope of the public domain of knowledge, even as they depend on new commercial arrangements based on authorial rights of the researcher and the university.

The third policy change is an internal proposal, which I expect to adopt this year, to formalize the submission of electronic theses and dissertations at UIC. We are obviously neither the first nor last to do this. And I am fond of pointing out that all dissertations at UIC are already electronic—we just insist on printing them out and putting bound copies in the library. Under our new policy, we will require that all dissertations be submitted in electronic form to the university and to ProQuest. We have not made a final decision about archival bound copies.

Perhaps most importantly, we will strengthen our system of mentoring and guidance so that students writing dissertations will have reasonable information about the decisions they face about the ownership and dissemination of their research. For example, we will not require students to release their dissertations via ProQuest, although the dissertations will be publicly available through our own library. However, we will not support extended embargoes of dissertations. While an author may wish to have a reasonable interval to secure patents, etc., we believe that a dissertation, as a key exercise within the academic discourse community, should be open and accessible within our community.

There may be obstacles, however, to broader distribution. A dissertation in the humanities, for instance, faces sharply reduced chances of acceptance by a university press if it is already available on the internet. And a dissertation in the sciences may already be under partial copyright by journal publishers.

As scholars and doctoral students seek to negotiate this complex landscape, they face shifting ideas of authorship and of plagiarism. I recently heard an anecdote about a Nobel prize-winner accusing a dissertation writer of plagiarism because some of the material had already appeared in an article. (What matters about the story is not whether it was true but whether it was believed). To my understanding, the author in this case might be accused of being boringly repetitious or devoid of new ideas or of padding his resumé, but not of being a plagiarist. (Disclosure: I am the writer of a book whose "Author," via the publisher's contract, is a research library. I retain the right to quote 80% of the book at one time, but I am not free to quote all of myself all of the time.)

If there is some trouble over the conditions in which a dissertation writer can use his or her own work, there is likewise some contradiction in how the student may use the work of others. Most dissertations in the sciences are in significant ways collaborative efforts. (Indeed, as a humanist, I often argue that too few humanities dissertations are collaborative efforts.) Successful scientists generally work in groups, with high levels of collaboration across institutions and national boundaries. Hence invention and authorship are multiple and the origination of ideas is often difficult to pinpoint—even as the fear of having one's ideas stolen is increased by their ease of transmission. At a doctoral defense, the dissertation is certified by a faculty committee and by the graduate dean as an original contribution to knowledge by the student, even as its chapters are being published in journals as the work of multiple collaborators.

This contradiction between the idea of proprietary authorship on the one hand and, on the other, the fact of group production and need for open consumption on the other, generates some of the accusations of plagiarism and misappropriation that we are most familiar with.

If you ask graduate students what they think is the most rampant form of intellectual dishonesty, they commonly will say that it is the action of professors misappropriating the work of students. The students are hyper-aware of the incentives for their professors: the ability to win grants, pay raises and promotions, and to control intellectual property that might be taken to market. They are less sensitive to the perceptions of principal investigators that the PI has provided the funds, the lab, the major intellectual ideas, and the mentoring that the student needs to produce his or her work.

The struggle between graduate student and PI for intellectual ownership sometimes creates situations where the PI won't sign off on the dissertation until the student completes additional experiments that may lie outside the scope of the dissertation, or places the dissertation chapters for publication in journals, even though the originality, accuracy, or intellectual quality of the work is neither increased nor decreased by the fact of acceptance. I have been confronted with situations where a journal tries to refuse permission to a student to reprint an article within the dissertation if it is reformatted to meet the university's standards.

Recently I heard a story—again what matters is the fact that it was believed—that inverts this scenario in a startling way. Instead of preventing the student from finishing, some very prominent PI's in very prominent labs—according to this anecdote—have actually finished their students' dissertations for them. If true, this is an odd sort of misbehavior, but it is possible to construct a motive. With the rise of project grants, a super-PI needs collaborators who are strong enough to be direct portions of the project, but not so strong that they wish full independence. The easiest way to achieve this is to grow your own, which shifts the PI's incentive from wanting the student not to finish to wanting the student to finish. This behavior is—according to the story—an open secret within the group, but a secret where all benefit by sharing.

In the face of powerful incentives to individual and group misconduct, our received, deeply-conflicted, western post-romantic ideas of authorship are simply inadequate. The inscription of these conflicted ideas within national legal codes will not resolve the issues, nor will the imposition of one national legal culture onto others. The cultural forces at work are too complex and too heterogeneous to admit of legislative solutions that will not become obsolete quickly. I say this because the cultural forces that underlie what I have described are not simply those of national or ethnic cultures, but of at least six different cultural dimensions that intersect in any research-university laboratory:

- ethnic or national culture
- generational culture
- culture of gender
- academic disciplinary culture
- academic institutional culture
- national regulatory regime

The only serious approaches are, in my estimation, "glocal," that is, they are actions that originate at the most local level of the individual lab, institution, association etc. up the scalar ladder, and that are consistent with the fundamental forces of globalization. At the "local" level, the laboratory, institution and discipline need to recognize themselves as new cultural creations in their own right and act as sites of a globalizing synthesis. That is, the collaborative work within a lab of individuals of, say, Indian, Chinese, American and European origin does not add their cultural assumptions together but mutually challenges them to rethink the bases for their assumptions.

At the global level, we see great pressure on post-romantic notions of individual authorship and authorial property through the forces of accelerated global flows of capital—financial, intellectual, and human.

Financial capital now flows easily across borders and legal and regulatory regimes in the form of equity, debt, and derivatives thereof, often in ingeniously designed packages such as CDO's and default swaps. (Recent events suggest that the flow has been too easy and the forms too ingenious.) Intellectual capital likewise flows easily with electronic publication and increasingly, with pre-publication circulations of new findings. The flow of human capital has similarly accelerated, with large population migrations within nations as global urbanization accelerates, and with migration across national borders. The movement of intellectuals—whether faculty or students— across national boundaries represents a tiny fraction of this human movement, but a significant one when multiplied by the amount of human capital they carry.

The fundamental challenge to all of these global capital flows and global markets is the challenge of trust. In terms of intellectual capital, how do I know these ideas are "good," in the sense of verifiable and reliable? Can I act on them? With whom should I best cooperate or collaborate? The answer is: the "author," not in the simple sense of the person whose name is at the beginning of the words. That name may be fraudulent. Instead, we may revert to the early meaning of the Latin root, "auctor," a person who stood surety for a real estate deal during the Roman Republic. The "author" in this sense is the person or party who can best assure us that the ideas are good.

Universities play a critical role in this assurance. We are deeply involved not only in the creation of intellectual capital, but also in its conversion into financial capital through technology transfer, and its conversion into human capital via degrees. Just as a collateralized debt obligation is a bundle of notes that may be worthless one by one, but once bundled together properly and certified have a significantly lowered risk and become credit-worthy, so a graduate degree can be seen as a bundle of class and lab notes that have reached a sufficient scale and consistency to become credible. Likewise when we pass a dissertation or are involved in refereeing or publishing a scholarly article, we are certifying that the intellectual property in it is worthy of examination, and belongs to the individuals whose names appear as authors, and in some rough proportion to the sequence in which those names appear. And finally, when we participate in policies to strengthen public assess, we strengthen the transparency of the marketplace of ideas.

In this broad analysis, there exist in the complexity around us some emerging ways to align the incentives facing individual researchers and research groups with a shared academic public good. The antidote to academic misconduct may best lie in the promotion of enlightened self-interest, and the realization that trust—and trustworthiness—are the most valuable commodities.

# Electronic Publishing and Authorship Issues: The Australian Context

**Maxwell King**
**Pro Vice-Chancellor, Research and Research Training**
**Monash University**

## Electronic Publishing of Theses

Until recently, Australian universities only required that the theses of their successful students be lodged in the library. Hence the only place one could be sure a particular thesis could be found was the university library. There was a feeling that the thesis was read by very few people, certainly the supervisor and the examiners and perhaps one or two students who were studying in a similar area.

About five years ago the Australian Government began advocating greater access to research output particularly for research paid for by the Government. They funded a range of projects aimed to develop electronic research repositories and the Australian Digital Thesis Project. The latter has encouraged most universities to require students to provide an electronic version of their theses in addition to the paper versions used for examination purposes.

A major debate going on in many Australian universities at present is whether to "publish" such theses on their websites. Arguments in favour are that the outcome of such research should be publicly available. Also, open access to such theses would make them more likely to be cited and acknowledged by the literature. They do provide knowledge that without publication on the web it might be lost to the community, particularly in cases where students do not go on to academic or research related careers.

There are minor issues, such as the need to require our students to obtain copyright clearance for any tables, diagrams, artwork, etc., not their own, as well as quoted text beyond reasonable use. Students may also need to get copyright clearance for any published work of which they are an author that is included as part of the thesis. I have noticed that some commercial publishers are very willing to allow students to include published work in theses. For example, Elsevier include the following right of authors under their standard transfer of copyright agreement: "The right to include the article in full or in part in a thesis or dissertation provided that this is not to be published commercially."

A more troubling complaint raised by some students and their supervisors is that having the work available through open access might make it harder to publish. Also, some students join research teams in which background intellectual property is made available and new intellectual property is therefore co-owned. The co-owners may not wish the thesis to be published online immediately. One solution is to allow such work to be embargoed for a set period, typically for up to three years.

Generally speaking, we are asking both students and to a lesser extent supervisors to do extra work, but we think the outcomes make this worthwhile.

## Authorship Issues

I have held the role of Dean of Graduate Studies or its equivalent at Monash University for just over 15 years. In my experience the number of research students who are raising issues of authorship is increasing. I think this is in part due to an increase in the number of co-authored papers and an increase in the number of co-authors on an average paper. I recently had to interview a number of senior colleagues in our Faculty of Medicine, Nursing and Health Sciences concerning a complaint regarding authorship practices. As a result it has become very clear to me that different disciplines can have quite different authorship cultures. What seems to be regarded as grounds for being named as an author on a clinical medicine paper might not be recognised as grounds for authorship in the humanities and perhaps many parts of the social sciences.

It might be that we could reduce the number of disputes about authorship if we could document in some detail how authorship should be decided. Unfortunately these clear cultural differences cause great difficulties when it comes to writing an institutional code for authorship. Because a variety of practices have to be covered, such institutional codes are typically lacking in detail, or at least the kind of detail new researchers would find helpful. I feel this is an issue that needs further work on our parts.

# VI. PROMISING COLLABORATIONS

## Summary of Presentations and Group Discussion:

The final theme-based session took the earlier discussion on "best practices" in a new direction: participants discussed some of the strategies that have been used for collaboratively supporting scholarly integrity in a global context. The session was organized around three topics.

For the first part, **John Hayton** of Australian Education International and **Catharine Stimpson** of NYU (in abstentia), addressed the question, **"What are the concrete issues upon which international collaborations are most needed or possible?"** John Hayton outlined a number of areas for future work, including improving administrative structures for diffusing information about scholarly integrity to national organizations. In addition, he listed a number of specific topics needing further assessment and recommended an outcomes-based approach: examining teaching methods to ensure that they help students learn effectively; considering the role of English in graduate education and ensuring that other languages are included and preserved; and learning how better to include minorities and other under-represented groups. In the discussion following this presentation, additional attention was given to measuring the outcomes of educational experiences that affect a student's perspective on scholarly integrity. For example, **Adriano De Maio** of the University of Milan noted that it would be useful to measure the long-term effects of international study on students, since this experience can change a student's cultural perspective (and ability to relate to different ethical frameworks). There was also interest in measuring the effectiveness of different methodologies for teaching ethics.

The second part of the session focused on the **best existing examples of international partnerships**. **Shi-Gang Sun** of Xiamen University discussed steps taken in China to promote internationalization of higher education, giving special focus to efforts to coordinate the work of universities and the government. **Barbara Evans** of the University of British Columbia discussed the recent work of Universitas 21, a network of universities that has sought to educate students about scholarly integrity in a specifically global context. In particular, this program seeks to create common definitions of concepts related to scholarly integrity, Dr. Evans explained, but it also helps students understand that ethical beliefs are often rooted in culture. It is also designed to help students reflect on the dilemmas that may arise when individuals are bound to different and conflicting sets of ethical rules.

The last discussion focused on the **role of national and international associations and organizations in facilitating international collaborations**. **Mandy Thomas** of the Australian National University underlined the need of such institutions to go beyond training initiatives to make broader-based efforts to raise awareness about issues of scholarly integrity and to build stronger research cultures. (One approach mentioned by Dr. Thomas was to support scholarly integrity as a professional value, by asking questions about research integrity in job interviews). Both Dr. Thomas and **Karen DePauw** of Virginia Tech also supported improved coordination among organizations that play a key role in shaping university research cultures. Dr. DePauw concluded the session by providing an overview of the areas that need focused future attention on the part of national and international institutions, including classified research, patent policy, copyright issues, human subjects research and animal welfare, national and international legal issues.

Because the approaches described here are collaborative, they are also the most complex, requiring coordination both within and between institutions. It is for this reason that they merit particularly sustained and active communication in the future.

# What Are the Concrete Issues upon Which International Collaborations Are Most Needed or Possible?

Catharine R. Stimpson
Dean, Graduate School of Arts and Science
New York University

John TW Hayton
Counsellor (Education), Australian Education International-North
America
Embassy of Australia

Our topic is "What are the concrete issues upon which international collaborations are most needed or possible?" We will first sketch out, far too briefly, the context in which such issues arise. We will then suggest some scholarly questions that call out for collaborative research and teaching, and next, some institutional questions. Finally, we will end with a statement of broad principles that can govern our common explorations. We have not been comprehensive. We do not pretend that we are offering a complete tour of the horizon. Instead, we hope to stimulate a helpful conversation.

## The Context:

It is now utterly banal to say that we all live in a globalizing world. It is far less banal to describe the multiple institutions and networks that exist within globalization. Some are transnational; some are regional; some are national; some are provincial or states within a nation such as Tasmania within Australia or Washington within the United States; some are county or city-wide. The stakeholders in this discussion include those directly involved in graduate education and also employers and governments. The broad objectives in this discussion include the growth of knowledge, the support of innovation, the building of new activities and structures, and the economic growth that will underpin our society's ability to nurture education. For some institutions the discussion will be grounded in building upon excellence, in others building capacity, and for all a shared understanding of what quality might mean.

This fundamental multiplicity affects graduate education. That is, graduate education exists on each and every one of these levels. One, and only one consequence, is that our discussions about graduate education do and will take place at multiple levels and at multiple sites. We can have all the "global" conversations we want, but we must have all the conversations at multiple levels and at multiple sites that we need. Moreover, our conversations— at every level and site— must balance the forces of collaboration and competition. When Australian John and American Catharine sit together at a conference table, they are only too aware that faculty members in their countries read each other's work, do research together, belong to the same chat-rooms, and attend conferences together. Australian John and American Catharine are also only too aware that their countries are battling it out, peacefully, for international students at their national colleges and universities.

Our ethical task is to encourage the collaborations, to support a broader international understanding of graduate education, consider frameworks that would enable an understanding of the quality of provision and the way institutions assure that quality, and to keep the competition within the bounds of law and civility. As collaborators and competitors, we must all be keenly aware that not all institutions of higher education and graduate education are alike. To be sure, we have a common sense of the structure of graduate education and its hierarchy of master's degrees, doctoral degrees, and postdoctoral degrees. However, some have far more resources than others. Some are far more committed to equity than others. Some are far more dependent on government's support than others. Some must struggle more arduously with corruption than others.

## The Scholarly Issues:

Graduate education has several ambitions, but research and scholarship are primary among them. Researchers and scholars are the most appropriate source of the scholarly questions on which collaborations can most fruitfully take place. Indeed, researchers and scholars have a long, deep tradition of collaborations, be they disciplinary or interdisciplinary. Human survival rests on the strength of collaborative research into diseases, the environment, global climate change, and the spread of nuclear and biological weaponry. At the risk of temerity and narrowness, let us suggest some concrete scholarly issues that focus on graduate education. One is the causes and consequences of the multiple differences we noted so quickly above. (*Towards a Global Ph.D.: Forces and Forms in Doctoral Education Worldwide*, which Maresi Nerad and Mimi Heggelund edited in 2008, is a helpful text).

We can ask how graduate institutions are working with the "minority" populations among their actual and potential students. A compatible question is how elite institutions are serving less privileged ones. If we have democratic values, we must think about educating everyone— not just future leaders. If we take on this task, how do we assess teaching and learning without establishing really rigid, boring, exclusively quantitative measures? Will English continue to be the global natural language of scholarship, research, and graduate education? Whether it is or not, do we not have a responsibility to help maintain local languages and to learn other global languages? Why shouldn't all graduate students learn some math and statistics? Underlying these specific researchable questions is an ethical question: what are the ethical conditions of graduate education? How do people concerned with graduate education globally vibrantly define these conditions (for us, they include academic freedom, integrity, freedom from harassment, and equity) and then sustain them?

## The Institutional Issues

Quite deliberately, we have outlined some scholarly issues that in part focus on institutions. The findings that researchers and scholars give us will help with two crucial issues about institutional well-being. One concerns the best mediums for the exchange of best practices (or even O.K. practices). In other words, does everyone have to talk to everyone about everything? Or do we need more focussed conversations among well-defined affinity groups? The second concerns the nature, meaning, and purposes of the master's degree. We would suggest that the master's degree is less well understood and less well articulated than the baccalaureate or the doctoral degree. This is because of its relative newness on global and national stages, because of its rapid growth, and, in terms of Europe, its interesting place in the Bologna Process.

## A Statement of Principles

Collaborations, like all human arrangements, can be excellent, good enough, and bad. Like all human arrangements, they can be long-lasting, seasonal, or as short as the Arctic summer. We enter into them because we are convinced, with varying degrees of clear-sightedness, that the whole will be more than the sum of its parts. Whether bilateral or multilateral, collaborations should embody five principles: 1) They are rooted in solid, shared academic values. 2) Partnerships reflect a clear and lucidly articulated sense of mutual interests.

For example, academic partnerships between North America and Europe can usefully do comparative studies of modern empires. 3) Partnerships emanate mutual respect, much more than lip service to the strengths, promise, and value of the Other, whether that Other be an institution or a person. 4) Partnerships are sustainable financially, and richer institutions have an obligation to contribute more to sustainability than poorer ones; and 5) Partnerships are administratively supple, smooth, and competent, and as such, can include benchmarks and exit strategies.

Some of Catherine R. Stimpson's remarks are adapted from her speech "European Higher Education Viewed from Outside" given at the ACA Annual Conference, Tallinn Estonia 17 June 2008.

# The State of Internationalization of Post-Graduate Education at Xiamen University

### Shi-Gang Sun
### Vice-President and Dean of the Graduate School
### Xiamen University

## The State of Internationalization at Xiamen University

Xiamen University places great emphasis on its internationalization process. At the outset of the establishment of Xiamen University, the school clearly stated in its Mission Statements that the aim of the university is to probe into the essence of each phenomenon and to explore the inner beauty of Chinese civilization by drawing on academic resources of all nations, so as to shape the most cutting-edge and complete cultures of the university. Since its founding, Xiamen University has adhered to the concept of an open mode of school-running, launching a full-range of international and regional academic exchanges and cooperation. It has set up intercollegiate relationships with 142 universities from countries such as the USA, the UK, Japan, Russia, France, Germany, Canada, Australia, Holland, Philippine, South Korea, Thailand, and from regions of Hong Kong, Taiwan and Macao; in the meantime it has carried out various academic exchanges with numerous research institutes at home and abroad. In order to broaden the international perspective of its students, the university has employed a group of world-renowned scholars as its honorary professors and visiting professors, including Chen Ning Yang (otherwise known as Yang Zhengning) and Tsung-Dao Lee (otherwise known as Li Zhengdao), to teach at the university, conduct academic workshops or engage in co-studies at the university. Since 1980, more than 2,000 foreign experts have come to Xiamen University for teaching, lecturing or research, and the university has successfully held over 200 international academic conferences. In addition, Xiamen University has established partnerships in education and scientific research with ten overseas universities. In April, 2004, the university signed the joint agreement, "Global U8 Consortium," with Inha University of South Korea, the University of Rhode Island of the U.S., the University of Washington of the U.S., La Havre University of France, the University of Haifa of Israel, the Royal Melbourne Institute of Technology of Australia, and Meiji University of Japan (which joined the consortium in 2005). In 2007, the University of Hull of the U.K. and the University of Hawaii of the U.S.

also became members of the consortium. In terms of cross-Taiwan Strait communication, Xiamen University enjoys a unique geological location and cultural advantages; it has carried out academic exchanges and established cooperative relationships with dozens of universities and research institutes in Taiwan, making itself the most active university on the Chinese mainland with regard to cross-Strait communication in the field of education, science and technology, and cultural exchanges. Meanwhile, the university has hosted various high-level cross-Strait academic seminars, organized friendship-bonding activities for youth from both sides of the Taiwan Strait, and conducted co-studies on certain subjects with colleges, universities and research institutes in Taiwan, thus upgrading the level of disciplinary construction and scientific research at the university.

In recent years, as the internationalization process of the university advances further and its accompanying measures are reinforced, there follows a quickening trend of post-graduates going abroad for academic exchanges. The school encourages graduate students to actively engage in international academic exchanges by creating a favorable environment for academic exchanges. In other words, the purpose of internationalization is to create more opportunities for those excellent post-graduates to study the state-of-the-art academic thoughts and advanced experimental techniques in renowned foreign universities and research institutes. At present, the international exchange programs offered by the university include cooperation in scientific research, academic exchanges, participation in international conferences, state-funded oversea study programs, joint education of post-graduates with universities outside the Chinese mainland, oversea study, intercollegiate exchanges of students, scientific expeditions and teaching Mandarin abroad.

## Post-Graduates of Xiamen University Pursuing Study Overseas

In terms of the scale of oversea study, since 2005, the number of post-graduates pursuing study outside the Chinese mainland while keeping their student status at Xiamen University stands at 491, of which the number of doctoral students is 210, accounting for 15% of the total doctoral students, and that of master's students is 281, accounting for 3.8% of the total master's students.

In terms of programs, the number of students traveling abroad for international conferences is 103; for joint education it is 104, for academic exchanges 118, for intercollegiate exchanges 43, and for other programs 83, with the numbers adding up to 92% of the total number of students studying abroad. Among them, 67% of the doctoral students are traveling overseas for the purpose of participating in international conferences and joint education; 55% of the master's students are going abroad for the purpose of academic exchanges (72 of them) and there are also students participating in other programs (83 of them).

Since 2005, the number of post-graduates studying overseas has been rising year by year and the international program has become more diversified. In 2005, the number of international post-graduates maintained at merely 26, and mainly included students pursuing academic exchanges; in 2006, the number reached 49, and mainly included students pursuing academic exchanges and joint education, an 88% increase over the same period of 2005; in 2007, this figure rose to 238, a year-on-year increase of 394% over 2006, and the purpose of this group was more diversified, including academic exchanges, international conferences, joint education and intercollegiate student exchange. Since January, 2008, the number of international post-graduates has gone up to 154.

The rapid growth of post-graduates studying overseas is attributed to the strengthened input of the state into the state-funded international programs for post-graduates and to the deepening communication between the university and its international partners in recent years. Further input is coming. In order to meet the demand of the state for high-level creative talents and to strengthen the implementation of the national strategy of reinvigorating China through human resource development, the state will considerably expand the scale of post-graduates on state-funded international programs during its Eleven Five-year Plan (from 2006 to 2010). The Ministry of Education requires that each university or institute make full use of educational resources at home and abroad, with the emphasis on putting into full play its current international cooperation and exchanges, and international programs offered by China Scholarship Council. With the advancement of the internationalization process, the level of international exchange pursued by post-graduates of the university will be further enhanced; the horizons of our post-graduates will be further broadened; and the quality of our post-graduates education will be further improved.

## The Enrollment of International Students at Xiamen University

With its favorable geological location on the west coast of the Taiwan Strait, its beautiful scenery and rich cultural resources on the campus, Xiamen University is an ideal place for students to pursue their study. Receiving international students is an important part of international cooperation and university exchange. Xiamen University is proud to have produced the first international doctoral student majoring in oceanography and first international doctoral student specializing in accounting in China. It consistently follows the guideline of expanding the scale of international students, aiming for a higher level of exchanges, ensuring the quality of education and standardizing the management of international students, which is stipulated by the Ministry of Education, to carry out its work on international cooperation. It exerts itself to expand the channel for international students to come to Xiamen University for study by encouraging and inviting foreign governments and Chinese enterprises to set up scholarships for international students. To ensure the quality of education for international students, the university strives to improve the mechanism of expert consultancy on studying at Xiamen University and to make full preparation for accepting international students. In the context of China's growing national strength and years of development and experience in receiving international students, the university is attracting more and more international students to pursue study here, resulting in an increasing number of students coming to Xiamen University for master's and doctoral degrees.

Post-graduates, who come to Xiamen University for further study, include foreign master's and doctoral students, and master's and doctoral students from Hong Kong, Macao and Taiwan. Between 2005 and 2007, the university received 257 post-graduates, of whom 163 were master's students, accounting for 63% of the total, and 94 were doctoral students, accounting for 37% of the total. In terms of their places of origin, 153 of them were of foreign nationality, 60% of the total, and 104 of them were from Hong Kong, Macao and Taiwan, 40% of the total.

International students who pursue study in China either study at their own expense or on a full scholarship. Between 2005 and 2007, the number of self-financing international students stood at 210, accounting for 82% of the total, and the number of students granted a full scholarship reached 47, 18% of the total.

Through the promotion of its international programs in the past three years, the university has witnessed a rising number of international post-graduates. In 2005, there were 45 international students in the university; in 2006 the number rose to 76, an increase of 69% over the same period of 2005; in 2007, it went up to 136, a year-on-year increase of 79%.

## International Master's Programs Offered by Xiamen University

With the goal of boosting its internationalization process, starting from 2007,

Xiamen University has launched international master's programs in its School of Humanities, School of Law, School of Economics, College of Oceanography and Environmental Science, College of Chemistry and Chemical Engineering, and School of Life Sciences, seeing an enrollment of 47 in the first batch of students. These international master's programs, which are all conducted in English, aim to produce high-level international professionals who not only build a solid foundation in their specialized fields, but also emerge fully equipped with knowledge of Chinese society and cultures. In 2008, supported by the Chinese Government Scholarship, Xiamen University begins its enrollment of students in seven more international master's programs, including Chinese Cultures, Chinese Civil and Commercial Law, Asia-Pacific International Relations, Chinese Economy, Biochemistry and Molecular Biology, and Chemical Engineering. 77 foreign students from 21 countries, distributed among 25 master's and doctoral programs, were admitted to these programs.

# The Universitas 21 Program in Global Research Ethics and Integrity

**Barbara Evans**
**Dean of Graduate Studies**
**University of British Columbia**

This program is provided as an example of an existing international network recognizing its responsibility to provide leadership in education about scholarly integrity and research ethics in a global context, and working effectively to develop a shared curricular resource on this topic for its graduate students.

## The Universitas 21 Consortium

This program was the initiative of Graduate Deans from Universitas 21 (U21)– an international network of research-intensive universities from 21 countries. The program was designed to engage graduate students in the consideration of issues related to research ethics and scholarly integrity in a global context and to reflect on the ways that personal, institutional, regulatory and cultural perspectives interact in the practice of ethical behavior. The development group comprised representatives from nine member universities– Birmingham, Edinburgh, Hong Kong, Lund, Melbourne, New South Wales, Nottingham, Queensland and Virginia, and the project was funded by the U21 network. It was then "created" by a team at The University of Melbourne.

The main goal of the U21 Deans & Directors of Graduate Studies (DDOGS) group is to work together to achieve advances in graduate education for all graduate students. To this end the following questions were posed: "What important *attributes* should be expected of **all** graduate students around the world?"; "Which of these could be achieved most effectively by an international network of like universities such as U21?"; "How could we collaborate to ensure that our students are provided with the best possible opportunities to be aware of and develop these attributes?

It was decided that *'a personal understanding of and commitment to integrity and ethical behavior in an international context'* was:

* one of the most important of these attributes,
* highly relevant to **all** students whether they continued in research or academia or whether they would be one of the other half of

our graduates who work in business, industry, government or other activities, and

• an attribute that demanded broad consideration in a global context rather than simply from the perspective of local compliance.

## Who is it for?

The program was designed to be undertaken by graduate students at either master's or doctoral levels. It is somewhat focused towards those actually undertaking a research project as part of their academic program but it is expected that it would also be valuable for students undertaking coursework and professional programs.

For those who need to submit an ethics application, the program provides insight into issues considered by university ethics committees. Even those whose research doesn't require ethics approval will be asked to reflect on high-level ethical dilemmas facing the modern researcher.

The final section of the program directs students to resources at their university if they are required to apply for ethics approval. The program also allows universities to tailor the program and include additional links to local regulations and requirements relevant to them.

## What was the perceived need for such a program?

It is increasingly recognized that it is the responsibility of universities to ensure that all researchers we train develop generic and professional skills that include integrity and ethical conduct. Our graduate students must have a sound grasp of both the nature of ethical concerns and the relevant ethics policies and procedures within their institution and country.

Many departments, faculties and institutions do provide some formal training in ethics, some require it, and most have clear regulatory and compliance requirements. However fewer appear to provide a broad program that encompasses the overarching principles and perspectives.

Canada's Tri-agency (representing the three major Canadian research funding agencies) prepared a "Statement of Principles on Key Professional Skills for Researchers" in 2007 which includes the following principle:

*"Integrity and ethical conduct– Researchers are aware of and adhere to professional codes of conduct and standards in and beyond their disciplines. They are sensitive to ethical considerations*

*in situations involving conflict of interest, appropriate authorship, and intellectual property attributions. They display impartiality and rigour when performing research and when analyzing and reporting research results. They are also sensitive to the ethical aspects of multidisciplinary and multicultural situations, taking into account social and environmental considerations.*

*Researchers demonstrate responsible conduct in research and adhere to the standards for academic citation in writing in specific disciplines. They are able to handle competing obligations ethically and to negotiate and manage ethical dilemmas. In addition, they are able to engage in critical analysis of rules and standards to ensure that they are fair and equitable."*[1]

There are also a number of excellent websites providing great resources on this topic, for example the U.S. Office of Research Integrity.[2]

## What does the program involve?

The program is web-based, interactive and ideally incorporates chat rooms, blogs and/or face-to-face workshops to ensure a thorough consideration of the ideas. Throughout the program, students are encouraged to discuss issues with their supervisors, particularly those that may be relevant to their own research. The program commences with an opening discussion to set the scene.

## Program Content

An opening discussion is followed by seven 'chapters' or 'hypotheticals' dealing with various ethical issues that cross disciplinary boundaries. The broad topics covered include: research governance, research conduct, authorship and IP, the limits of research methodologies, consent and confidentiality, working with indigenous communities, children and informed consent, community ethics, animal research and the commercialization of research. In this way, students are encouraged to reflect on issues such as

- the basic principles of ethical conduct: intellectual honesty, respect for others, justice, human rights, beneficence and risk minimization.
- the ways that culture, religion, gender and politics can affect one's ethical framework.
- the complexity of some ethical issues and how they may be regarded

differently in different national and international contexts.

- 'best' practice and cases where there seems to be no 'right' or 'wrong' answers, even though there are certain ethical mores to which most cultures and religions subscribe.
- the differing responsibilities of student researchers, supervisors, universities and governments (who are usually responsible for policy and regulation of ethical matters).
- their responsibility as a highly educated member of the community to demonstrate integrity and behave ethically.

## Website and Activities

Each *case study* is intended to elicit responses to hypothetical ethical dilemmas. Activities including Reflections, Research Tasks, Further Reading, Podcasts and Videos help the student engage fully with the material.

*Research Tasks* require students to complete any additional reading or research as suggested and then write their responses in the space provided.

*Reflections* require students to consider their personal responses to the issues raised in each case study. They may choose to revise these thoughts after having worked through later chapters. It is suggested that a useful way to engage with the ideas presented is to write from all possible perspectives of key players or subjects, while ensuring familiarity with the code of conduct of the student's university.

*Further Reading* includes reference data for each case study or more background material to help the student understand the topic in greater depth.

*Podcasts* – students should listen to podcasts and take notes to improve their active listening skills.

*Video controls* – students may watch a number of videos throughout the program and/or read the transcript provided as a link below.

*Resources* – a Resources tab provides further references for delving more deeply into the issues.

*Evaluation* – students are requested to complete an evaluation, which should take 10-15 minutes. The information so provided will be used to evaluate the program and improve its content and operation.

## References

1   http://www.tss.uoguelph.ca/pdfs/ProfSkills4Researchers.pdf

2   http://ori.dhhs.gov/education/rcr_resources.shtml

# *Promising Collaborations*

### Mandy Thomas
### Pro Vice-Chancellor
### The Australian National University

## What role should national or international associations and organizations play to facilitate international collaborations?

Collaboration in this context refers to be the ability of nations with a developed research integrity system to collaborate with nations with differing policy frameworks through education and research. The collaboration could involve co-operative training of students and academic staff in research integrity or developing 'top-down' shared frameworks and policies.

There is significant variation between countries in relation to commonly accepted research practices and policies guiding research. Recent international workshops on research integrity highlighted the fact that there is no common definition world-wide for what constitutes research misconduct; nor are there common rules for authorship, conflict of interest, plagiarism or numerous other terms with which one might determine what is acceptable or unacceptable research practice. Both national and international associations can play a key role in creating research training programs and in harmonizing definitions, standards and policies. These international bodies could also provide information on different practices, policy frameworks and governance structures for ethics and integrity around the world as well as inform institutions about best practice training methods on these issues. However if there is to be more global co-operation in training on research integrity matters there also needs to be more co-operation around dealing with cases of misconduct.

## Background

- There is growing recognition that the increasing global and collaborative nature of research activity demands a coordinated international effort to ensure high standards of integrity in research, and excellence in training. Due to the large investment in the research sector and its importance for stimulating economic growth, governments around the globe are also increasingly driven to ensure they have high national standards of integrity in research and can prevent research misconduct.

- Recognising the importance of this issue, the Organisation for Economic Co-Operation and Development's (OECD) Global Science Forum organized a Global Science Forum Workshop on best practices for ensuring scientific integrity and preventing misconduct in Tokyo in February of 2007. The workshop indicated that most OECD countries are developing stronger national processes for dealing with research misconduct although there is a spectrum of national responses from weak to strong. Many of the countries which do not yet have guidelines or a national agency to educate researchers about responsible research conduct are moving in the direction of national codes and setting up national offices of research integrity.

- The workshop participants proposed the development of an OECD statement on best practice in research integrity. This would involve: defining research misconduct; outlining the consequences of misconduct; and developing a set of overarching principles in responsible research practice and in dealing with research misconduct.

- Continuing the trend of growing global interest in collaborating on research integrity issues, a workshop was held on 'Fostering Responsible Research' in Lisbon, September 2007, with sponsorship from the European Science Foundation (ESF) and the U.S. Office of Research Integrity (ORI).

- Both workshops indicated that to have an impact beyond the policy domain, global standards for best practice and policies for responding to misconduct must be better incorporated into training and researchers must be better informed about policies.

- Effective collaboration promoting global responsibility must begin at the national level. As there is no universally agreed model process for dealing with allegations, when dealing with cases of misconduct in international collaborations, there needs to be funding provided by national governments to support involvement in global discussions and in co-operation on actual investigations.

## An International Approach

- A focus on collaborating on education cannot be effective if it is the only area of collaboration in research integrity matters. Increasing awareness of research integrity issues across the global research community is a foundational step prior to the development of broad-based global training policies. Also important is a global framework for dealing with research misconduct.

- There is some evidence that misconduct that occurs within international collaborative research projects is an especially difficult problem to address due to a lack of international agreement between funding agencies and governments on definitions, standards and procedures. Conducting enquiries across national boundaries also presents problems because of language barriers, different jurisdictional frameworks and the absence of formal agreements about dealing with misconduct.

- An outcome of the recent Lisbon conference was the recommendation for ESF and ORI to develop a *Global Clearing House for Research Integrity*. This clearing house will be in the form of a Wikipedia-style website built and added to by the global research community. It would provide general information on each nation's research conduct/misconduct policies; responsible conduct of research training programs; national and regional conferences and other related activities; and national and organisational research integrity contacts.

- There is a need for countries to develop generic models for documents related to international co-operative agreements (such as when there is a sharing of research facilities, funding, supervision etc.) to accommodate research integrity issues. At the same time it is important to recognize that there are differences between national systems, so effort should be made to identify areas of agreement and difference within the agreements.

- Other bodies which could be involved include learned academies, professional academic bodies and research funding bodies.

The US Office of Research Integrity is something of a world model and has a capacity to play a significant role as a world leader in research integrity thinking and in the advancement of research integrity on a global scale, particularly in relation to the question of how countries should deal with research misconduct when it occurs.

## Conclusion

It is critical that the research sector worldwide address research integrity policy and processes and establish international best practice frameworks in order to retain public confidence and government investment in research. National learned academies, national research funding agencies, Offices of Research Integrity or their equivalent, and organizations like the OECD and ESF all must play a role in enhancing training in research integrity and ethics globally. At the same time there must be action taken to make definitions, policies and processes surrounding responsible research and research misconduct globally compatible. Continuing to support international dialogue on these issues through the OECD, ESF and the U.S. ORI is recommended as the best means of achieving these aims.

# Promising Collaborations: What Role Should National or International Associations and Organizations Play to Facilitate International Collaborations?

**Karen P. DePauw**
**Vice President and Dean for Graduate Education**
**Virginia Tech**

Collaborations for graduate education and research between universities across national borders have become more numerous in the last 20+ years. Faculty and graduate student exchanges, graduate education degrees and joint research projects are examples of collaborative initiatives. These developments are welcomed inasmuch as a global perspective on graduate education and research/ scholarship is not only desired but critical to the advancement of knowledge needed to address the complex issues facing a 21$^{st}$ century global society.

As collaborations emerge, national and international associations and organizations have a critical role to play– that of leadership. Given the cultural differences in graduate education and scholarship around the world, these organizations can play an important role in developing common understandings and in framing a positive agenda for ethics in graduate training and scholarly integrity. These associations could:

- assist with the development and clarification of terminology, guidelines and principles
- facilitate the dissemination of materials and policy statements as appropriate
- provide a means for clear communication across countries, with attention to language translation and cultural relevance
- assist with the resolution of conflicts as they might arise
- evaluate and manage resources
- share good practices with colleagues around the world
- utilize technology to assist with these efforts, including the development of a digital resource center, and more.

Throughout this seminar, colleagues have presented, discussed and highlighted similarities and differences across countries, raised challenges and proposed opportunities for graduate deans to contemplate and to consider. The associations must now take the lead in:

- Facilitating the definition of terms such as scholarly integrity, research integrity, research ethics, responsible conduct of research, and other terms that might be used, and identifying related components
- Compiling and sharing good practices for the preparation of the future professoriate in a global context
- Compiling and sharing good practices for the preparation of future career professionals for business and industry
- Identifying mechanisms for preventing and resolving possible conflicts (e.g., patent rights, authorship, grant funding) with and without legal implications
- Determining if and which policy statements should be developed
- Examining the global perspectives of quality graduate education including mentoring, advising, curricula, and more
- Facilitating discussions of research compliance and scholarly misconduct
- Assisting with the development of curricular materials in differing formats, languages, and cultural contexts
- Understanding academic freedom in global contexts

In addition to the topics above, it is clear that specific topics will need to be examined in relation to the global context such as:

- Classified research and national security issues
- Patent policy and procedures across countries
- Differing models for graduate education including employment relations
- Challenges of digital–electronic thesis/dissertation and copyright permissions, image manipulation, authorship, plagiarism prevention
- Human participants and protection of human subjects, animal research, scientific misconduct
- Data gathering, storage, & retrieval
- Legal issues including issues of national vs. international law

As graduate education and research efforts expand throughout the world, national and international associations will need to become more attentive to the challenges of facilitating and communicating clearly about ethical endeavors and the advancement of research integrity in a global context.

Institutions of higher education as well as associations serving graduate education worldwide have a responsibility to ensure that our graduates are well prepared to enter a diverse global world.

# VII. CONCLUSION: TOWARDS FURTHER COLLABORATION AMONG GLOBAL RESEARCH CULTURES

The now annual Strategic Leaders Global Summit on Graduate Education was created in the fall of 2007 to provide an inclusive global platform for discussion of best practices in the preparation of students in programs that award advanced degrees. The domain of best practice was meant to be comprehensive, covering all phases of graduate education, from the transition into graduate school, to the process and substance of training, to the development of graduate students into professionals. Issues related to the topic of this year's summit, scholarly integrity in a global context, emerge at all of these phases in a graduate student's career; for this reason, they present university leaders with many different contexts in which to strengthen their graduate communities. Our hope for the second summit was to share experiences about challenges and opportunities in developing scholarly integrity and attempt to converge on a set of general and specific "to do" items for the future. I conclude with a reflection on just how far we progressed toward achieving these goals.

One of the central challenges for the conference was to build common goals for research ethics while respecting differences among different research cultures worldwide. If discussion topics did not always lead to consensus, there was agreement about the critical role of institutions in addressing them. In particular, participants agreed about the importance of institutional leadership; the need to recognize research ethics as a key element in graduate training; and the need to explore institutional and national differences that arise within international collaborations. And in all cases there was agreement that university leaders can most effectively cultivate a common culture of research if they are familiar with the range of cultural backgrounds represented by their graduate students and faculty.

As participants looked toward practical approaches to these issues, many noted that a plan of action, accompanied by a theory of change and mechanisms for assessing progress and outcomes, was essential. In addition, they agreed that graduate schools should work to make scholarly integrity a more integral part of a graduate student's program, and to support this effort with greater emphasis on prevention. As many speakers noted, one way to focus on prevention is to create research communities that are strong across the board in their work to support the education and careers of both students and faculty. For example, while providing resources for career development may not at first appear to be related to ethics, support for structures like these can reduce the temptation to violate ethical norms.

Finally, the summit allowed university leaders to explore the effects of international dialogue on their own universities' ethical standards. As the discussions of this summit show, all institutions have something to learn from the challenges and solutions developed at institutions with very different research cultures. The process of clarifying one's ethical processes to institutions outside one's own culture can also provide us with the opportunity to reexamine values and procedures that have become second-nature, and to modify and strengthen them.

Scholarly integrity and the preparation of scholars for the responsible conduct of research is a tough topic to make the focal point of an international dialogue. Yet the fact that a group of leaders from 10 countries was willing to commit to engage in the discussions should itself count as a successful outcome. One tangible measure of success for the Global Summit is the extent to which all participants coalesced around guidelines for future collaborations on the "best practice" area under discussion. It was gratifying to watch the convergence of this diverse group of leaders around a concrete set of understandings about shared challenges, leadership, communication and specific action items to be pursued. The strategic leaders from the countries represented in Florence firmly endorsed their consensus on these points as reflected in the document "Scholarly Integrity in a Global Context: Guidelines for Future Collaborations" (see Appendix A).

The capacity of institutions from around the globe to move knowledge forward hinges fundamentally on the integrity of the scholarship that undergirds that knowledge. And a country's capacity to ensure that integrity hinges in the first instance on the training and formation of young researchers. The guidelines for scholarly integrity forged at the Second Annual Strategic Leaders Global Summit on Graduate Education are a testimonial to the possibility that leaders of research and training worldwide are willing to work together to ensure that the best practices in advancing integrity programs will evolve with changing international cultures.

Debra W. Stewart
President
Council of Graduate Schools

# APPENDIX A: GUIDELINES FOR FUTURE COLLABORATIONS

During the final session of the conference, participants reached a number of consensus points about values common to all university leaders and guidelines for future work. The first set of conclusions helped define the **scope of shared challenges** in scholarly integrity:

- Scholarly integrity is a core value of all universities and requires systematic attention.
- Challenges to scholarly integrity are universal, diverse and evolving.
- Issues of scholarly integrity cut across institutional, inter-cultural, and international contexts.

The strategic leaders also agreed on three **forms of leadership and communication** that are most needed for guiding future collaborations:

- A common frame of reference that addresses the continuum of educational and training objectives from scholarly integrity to compliance
- Leadership at all levels to prepare future scholars, researchers, and professionals to demonstrate integrity in all aspects of their careers as scholars and to meet powerful pressures that undermine integrity
- Exchange of best practices and resources (including codes of conduct, regulatory frameworks, curricular materials, and instruments for assessment and evaluation)

Finally, participants agreed on five **specific action items** that organizations and/or universities should consider as they enhance and pursue international collaborations:

- Build scholarly integrity into existing structures that prepare future faculty and future career professionals
- Develop and maintain an open source, online website for facilitating resource and best practice exchange

- Utilize international joint degree, dual degree, and other collaborative program structures for integrating educational activities to advance scholarly integrity
- Identify mechanisms that explicitly address:
  - Universal and global issues in scholarly integrity, and
  - Ethical issues that may arise from the mobility of scholars (including the priority issues of digital publishing and plagiarism in an international environment)
- Develop collaborative mechanisms for addressing plagiarism in an international context

# APPENDIX B: PARTICIPANT BIOGRAPHIES

**Eleanor Babco** serves as Senior Consultant for the Professional Master's Program and Associate Program Director for the Professional Science Master's (PSM) project at the Council of Graduate Schools. She prepares reports and articles on the PSM project, provides information and guidance to existing PSM programs and for the development of new programs, as well as makes presentations addressing some aspect of the PSM. In addition, she works with the Government Relations staff and the CGS President on special projects. She is the former Executive Director of the Commission on Professionals in Science and Technology, a nonprofit corporation in Washington, DC that collects, synthesizes, analyzes and disseminates reliable information about the science and engineering workforce in the United States. She received grants from the Alfred P. Sloan Foundation, the GE Foundation, and the National Science Foundation for special studies at CPST.

Ms. Babco was educated as a chemist at Immaculata College and Catholic University, but has devoted her professional career to the analysis and interpretation of education and employment data about scientists and engineers, with particular attention to women and underrepresented minorities, and has written and published extensively on these issues. She received the WEPAN-sponsored Betty Vetter Award for Research in 2001, was named an AWIS fellow in 2002, and is a member of the Kellogg Research Council, Office for Diversity and Community Partnership, at Harvard Medical School.

**Yvonne Carter** trained at St Mary's Hospital Medical School in London and was awarded an intercalated honours degree in Clinical Pharmacology and Neuroanatomy in 1980. She graduated in 1983 with a distinction in Obstetrics and Gynaecology. Having completed her General Practice Vocational Training Scheme in Liverpool, she became a Member of the Royal College of General Practitioners in 1987. In 1990, she was awarded a three year RCGP Research Training Fellowship and during this time was an Honorary Research Fellow at Keele University. The University of London accepted her Doctorate of Medicine in 1994. She was awarded Fellowship of the RCGP in the same year.

From 1992-6 Professor Carter held the post of Senior Clinical Lecturer at the Department of General Practice, University of Birmingham. She became the youngest Professor of General Practice and Primary Care in the UK when she took up post as Chair and Head of Department at Barts and the London,

Queen Mary's School of Medicine and Dentistry in 1996. Two years later she was elected as a founder Fellow of the Academy of Medical Sciences. In 2001, she became Head of the Division of Community Sciences and in 2002, following restructuring in the School, became Director of the Institute of Community Health Sciences.

Professor Carter was a Member of the Council of the RCGP from 1994-2004 (elected from 2000). Between 1995-6 she was the Clinical Director of the Quality Network; from 1995-7 she was a member of the Commissioning of Care Task Force and from 1998-2000 she was a member of the Health Inequalities Group. From 1996-2001 she held the role of Chairman of Research and was also a member of the Council's Executive Committee.

Professor Carter's recent national roles include being a Governor of the Health Foundation from 1999-2007. From 1999-2004 she chaired the commissioning panel for the NHS National Primary Care R&D awards. She has also been involved in the development of the DH strategy on Research Governance. She was a member of the Appraisal Committee of the National Institute for Clinical Excellence from 1998-2001 and a member of the National Screening Committee from 1999-2003.

Professor Carter was appointed as Dean of Warwick Medical School in October 2004, following her role as Vice-Dean of Leicester Warwick Medical Schools during the preceding year. In 2005/6 the General Medical Council recommended that Warwick should receive independent degree awarding status and this was formally implemented when the Medical Act was changed in May 2007. WMS is currently organized into three Institutes: Clinical Sciences; Health Sciences and Clinical Education. As Dean and Head of the Faculty of Medicine, Professor Carter is responsible for a devolved budget of circa £30 million with over 320 staff; 700 medical students and around 2,000 CPD students. In August 2007 she became a Pro-Vice-Chancellor at the University of Warwick with responsibility for Regional Engagement.

For the last 20 years, Professor Carter has worked as a practicing GP with deprived inner city communities in Liverpool, Birmingham, East London and more recently in Coventry. She is currently an academic GP and Honorary Consultant in Primary Care at Coventry Teaching PCT and a Non-Executive Director and Vice Chair at University Hospitals Coventry and Warwickshire NHS Trust. She is also Chair of the Comprehensive Local Research Network for West Midlands (South).

Professor Carter has a personal research track record in health services research and the evaluation of new models of service delivery. In 2000 she received an OBE in the Queen's Birthday Honours List for services to health service research. In 2004 she also received an Honorary Fellowship from Queen Mary, University of London for services to general practice and primary care. She is a current member of the MRC Health Services and Public Health Research Board College of Experts; the UK Healthcare Education Advisory Committee of HEFCE and is an elected member of the Council of the Academy of Medical Sciences and a member of the Clinical Academic Careers Sub-Committee. She is also a member of the General Medical Council's Quality Assurance of Basic Medical Education visiting team. In 2006 Professor Carter also won the CBI's First Woman of Science Award.

**Chong-Qing Cheng** is currently Vice-president at Nanjing University. He is also the dean of the graduate school of the university and is responsible for all matters related to graduate education. Originally trained in engineering, Cheng moved to the field of mathematics after receiving the doctoral degree of engineering in China, and has several years of working experience in Germany as a Humboldt fellow and at Northwestern and ETH-Zurich as a Visiting Professor. Having worked in the area of dynamical systems for twenty years, Dr. Cheng performs research that covers topics such as KAM theory, Arnold diffusion, variational method, and bifurcation theory. He holds the position of Cheungkong Professor of Mathematics.

**Adriano De Maio** graduated in Electronic Engineering (1964) from Politecnico di Milano, where he is now full professor of Innovation Management. He has also held the positions of Rector and President of Politecnico di Milano (1994-2002) and of Luiss Guido Carli in Rome (2002-2005), Commissioner at the National Council of Research (CNR), (2003-2004), Chairman of the Evaluation Committee of Public Research Centers and Advisor on the Committee to the Ministry for higher education reform (2002-2004). He has also served as President of TIME (an association of top-level European technical universities), (2000/2002), as member of the board of the Ecole Centrale Paris, where he received a Ph.D. honoris causa, and Chairman of the Investment Committee of the Next Venture Capital Fund. Dr. De Maio is author of several books and many articles regarding the management of innovation and research. At present is also Counselor to the Governor of Regione Lombardia on matters regarding higher education, research and innovation. He is also President of the Regional Institute of Research (IreR).

**Karen P. DePauw** is Vice President and Dean for Graduate Education and tenured Professor in the Departments of Sociology and Human Nutrition,

Foods & Exercise at Virginia Tech in Blacksburg, Virginia. Prior to employment at VT, she served 22 years on the faculty and as an administrator at Washington State University. Since her arrival at Virginia Tech, her major accomplishments include success in building a strong diverse graduate community, the establishment of the innovative Graduate Life Center (GLC), and the signature initiative known as Transformative Graduate Education (TGE). The VT Graduate School supports 6500 graduate students pursuing 78 masters and 62 doctoral degrees at multiple campuses throughout Virginia and at several international locations and has administrative responsibilities for academic programs, recruitment and retention, alumni relations, fundraising, student support services and much more. She was a founding member and Facilitator/Chair for the Virginia Council of Graduate School (VCGS), served as President of the Council of Southern Graduate Schools (CSGS), 2007-2008 and currently serves as Chair of the Board of Directors of the Council of Graduate Schools (CGS).

Dr. DePauw is an internationally recognized scholar in the fields of adapted physical activity, disability sport and disability studies. She has published extensively (75+ books, journal articles and chapters), presented keynote and scholar lectures (more than 150) around the world. At WSU and VT, she has served as major advisor for 40+ graduate students and served on 50+ committees. Her scholarship has focused on inclusion, equity issues, social construction of disability, and sociology of the body. In recognition of her scholarly contributions, she was elected as a member of the American Academy for Kinesiology & Physical Education (AAKPE) in 1997. Throughout her academic career, she has served in leadership positions for national and international associations, received numerous honors and awards and has worked extensively with the United States Olympic Committee, the International Paralympic Committee and the Olympic & Paralympic Congresses since 1981.

Dr. DePauw earned the A.B. in Sociology from Whittier College, M.S. in Special Education from California State University, Long Beach, and a Ph.D. in Kinesiology from Texas Woman's University. In the 1970s, she taught with the Los Angeles City and Los Angeles County Schools and California State University – Los Angeles before moving to Washington State University.

**Daniel D. Denecke** is Director of Best Practices at the Council of Graduate Schools. He received his Ph.D. from Johns Hopkins and has served as faculty at the University of Maryland, College Park and Georgetown University. He is co-author of *Ph.D. Completion and Attrition (2004)*, which reviews recent empirical studies on the topic, discusses the institutional factors that contribute to graduate-degree completion, and outlines salutary interventions and next steps for improving completion rates in graduate education. Dr. Denecke is currently directing the CGS Ph.D. Completion Project, sponsored by Pfizer Inc and the Ford Foundation, and manages the Preparing Future Faculty (PFF) National Office at CGS. As Program Manager for the PFF program, he has worked extensively with graduate deans, faculty, and program directors to promote and institutionalize professional development programs for doctoral students aspiring to faculty positions. He is currently serving as a CGS (Preparing Future Faculty) consultant to Oxford University's Centre for Excellence in Academic Preparation, and is working with universities and organizations in the United States to assess the potential impact of the European "Bologna Process" on U.S. graduate admissions processes. Dr. Denecke's personal research focuses on pedagogy, literature, and the rise of social science in nineteenth-century Britain.

**Barbara Evans** commenced her present appointment as Dean of the Faculty of Graduate Studies at the University of British Columbia in early November 2007. Prior to this time, Professor Evans was Pro Vice-Chancellor (Research Training) at The University of Melbourne, with particular responsibilities for the oversight of policy, management and quality assurance for research higher degree programs, postgraduate generic skills training and research supervision. Since 1997, Barbara had also been Dean of the School of Graduate Studies (SGS), which provides for over 3,000 PhD students and 10,000 graduate students across the University. In addition to administering the PhD degree program and certain Masters programs, the School provides a broad range of academic support and professional skills programs for all postgraduate students. The school has also been committed to quality assurance and has been actively involved in national and international benchmarking of research higher degree practices.

Under Barbara's leadership, the School's value-added programs and services for students and supervisors, its development role and ethos have been recognized internationally for their excellence in providing for graduate students in a changing international educational environment. Barbara has been an invited speaker at many international conferences focused on graduate and research higher degree education in the US, Canada, Europe and Asia, and has been invited to review Graduate Programs at several Australian and international universities.

Barbara was elected Convener of the Australian Deans and Directors of

Graduate Studies for 2005–06, and in early 2006, was nominated by her peers as Convener of the Universitas 21 Deans and Directors of Graduate Studies. In March 2007, Barbara hosted the second of three international workshops "Forces and Forms of Change in Doctoral Education" organized through the Center for Innovation and Research in Graduate Education at the University of Washington and the University of Melbourne, and funded by the Ford Foundation for 35 invited attendees, representing 16 countries. She was also an invited member of the first "Strategic Leaders Global Summits on Graduate Education" hosted by the Council of Graduate Schools in 2007, with representatives from Canada, Europe, Asia, Australia and the United States. These 'Summits' are focused on best practices in graduate education in a global context.

Originally a zoologist, Barbara's research was concerned with the development of a broad understanding of the biology of a wide range of animal species. Her work was characterized by an interdisciplinary approach using a wide range of experimental techniques ranging from histology, biochemistry and organ physiology through to the physiology of freely-moving animals and animal behavior. During this period she undertook several overseas research appointments in the UK and Canada to work with international collaborators in the field of comparative zoology and her research resulted in the publication of over 100 book chapters, research papers and conference proceedings.

Barbara is an author and editor of three award-winning Biology textbooks for senior secondary and tertiary students, each now in their fourth edition. She is also an Olympian, representing Australia in Gymnastics at the Tokyo Olympic Games 1964 and the World Championships Germany 1966.

**Pavel Exner** was born in 1946 in Prague and graduated in 1969 from the Charles University. From 1978 to 1990 he worked at the Joint Institute for Nuclear Research, Dubna, where he got his PhD and DSc degrees. Later he was a leader of a research team in the Czech Academy of Sciences and taught theoretical physics as a professor at the Charles University. Now he heads the Doppler Institute for Mathematical Physics and Applied Mathematics in Prague. He is interested in mathematical methods related to quantum systems, in particular, quantum waveguides and graphs, unstable systems and solvable models. He is also the author of three books and more than 150 research papers, co-founder of the QMath conference series, and was awarded JINR prize in theoretical physics and the Czech Physical Society medal. At present he serves as a vice-president of the European Mathematical Society and of IUPAP and as secretary of the International Association for Mathematical Physics. His current position is Scientific Director, Doppler Institute, Prague.

**Jeffery C. Gibeling** was appointed Dean of Graduate Studies at the University of California, Davis in August 2002. He oversees 87 graduate degree programs, of which more than one-half are organized as interdisciplinary graduate groups. He previously served as Chair of the Academic Senate at UC Davis and Executive Associate Dean of Graduate Studies. He joined the faculty at UC Davis as an Assistant Professor of Materials Science and Engineering in 1984. Professor Gibeling holds degrees in Mechanical Engineering and Materials Science and Engineering from Stanford University. He also worked as an Acting Assistant Professor and Senior Research Associate at Stanford from 1979 through 1984. Professor Gibeling is the author or coauthor of more than 85 publications on the mechanical properties of materials and has guided the thesis and dissertation work of 25 graduate students.

Dean Gibeling has promoted continuous improvements in information technology to enhance service of the Office of Graduate Studies to its clientele. He is also deeply committed to increasing the diversity of the graduate population at UC Davis. Under Dean Gibeling's leadership the Office of Graduate Studies has developed a comprehensive Professional Development program to ensure that graduate students complete their degrees and are prepared for successful careers. He has also devoted significant attention to the needs of postdoctoral scholars and established an award for Excellence in Postdoctoral Research. Dean Gibeling serves on the CGS Board of Directors, the Association of Graduate Schools Executive Committee, the GRE Board and the TOEFL Board.

**Mercedes de Grado** holds a PhD in Spanish Studies from the University of Durham, United Kingdom. She has taught Spanish Studies for more than fifteen years at various universities, both in the United States and the United Kingdom. Dr. de Grado has published extensively in the field of Gender Studies and Spanish Cultural Studies. Her work *Sirenas náufragas a la deriva: identidad y debate feminista en la narrativa de Adelaida García Morales* was awarded the *Isidra de Guzmán* research prize in Spain. The book was published in 2004 by Publicaciones del Ayuntamiento de Alcalá de Henares, Madrid. Her research interests are Gender and Cultural Studies, with a focus on post-Franco Spain.

Dr. de Grado's passion for research and publishing brought her to ProQuest, where she is the International Relationship Manager for Dissertations Publishing. In this new role, she is responsible for speaking to universities outside of North America about participating in the global database for comparative graduate research, ProQuest Dissertations and Theses (PQDT), formerly known as Dissertations Abstracts.

**Fred L. Hall** started August 1 2007 as the Vice-Provost (Graduate Education) and Dean of Graduate Studies at the University of Calgary, in Alberta, Canada. Prior to July 1, he had been the Dean of Graduate Studies at McMaster University in Ontario for eight years, and had earlier served six years as an Associate Dean of Graduate Studies there. He holds a tenured appointment in Civil Engineering at Calgary, and has numerous publications in the areas of freeway traffic flow theory, operations, and quality of service, and earlier on the impacts of transportation noise on residential communities. His most recent research leave was spent in part at the University of Melbourne's School of Graduate Studies where he conducted research on cross-national comparisons of aspects of doctoral education.

**John Hayton** was appointed Counsellor (Education, Science and Training) at the Australian Embassy in Washington DC in February 2007. Prior to John's appointment he was a Director of the Americas, Europe, Multilateral and VET Sector Policy Section, International Co-operation Branch within DEST since January 2004. John's career has spanned 18 years with the Department of Foreign Affairs and Trade including postings in Bangkok and New York and three years leading and implementing an information technology industry development program in Tasmania (2001-03). Until recently John was Presiding Member of the Board of The Friends' School in Hobart Tasmania. The Friends' School, with 1300 students from K-12, offers the IB as a program option for Year 11 and 12 students and uses the PYP.

**Clark Hulse** is Dean of the Graduate College at the University of Illinois at Chicago, and Associate Chancellor and Vice Provost for Graduate and Continuing Studies. At UIC he holds appointments as Professor of English and Art History, and has been Visiting Professor of Art History at Northwestern University and Interim Director of the Center for Renaissance Studies at the Newberry Library. His research specialties are Shakespeare, Renaissance literature, and visual culture. He is the author of four books, *Elizabeth I: Ruler and Legend* (University of Illinois Press, 2003*), Early Modern Visual Culture: Representation, Race and Empire in the English Renaissance* (with Peter Erickson) (University of Pennsylvania Press, 2000), *The Rule of Art: Literature and Painting in the Renaissance* (University of Chicago Press, 1990), and *Metamorphic Verse: The Elizabethan Minor Epic* (Princeton University Press, 1981) plus numerous articles.

Professor Hulse is a Guggenheim Fellow and National Endowment for the Humanities Fellow, and has received research grants from the British

Academy and the College Art Association. Active in the area of public humanities, he serves on the Boards of Directors of the Illinois Humanities Council and the Chicago Humanities Festival and has worked on projects with Chicago Shakespeare Theater. In 2003 he curated a multi-part exhibition commemorating the 400th anniversary of the death of Elizabeth I, including a physical exhibit at the Newberry Library, a 40-city traveling exhibition sponsored by the American Library Association, and an online exhibit. The project was named by NEH as one of the "Milestones" of its first forty years, and the online exhibition won the 2004 Lieb Prize for outstanding web exhibition from the Association of Research Libraries.

Since 2005 Hulse has also been project director for the Richard J. Daley Urban Forum at UIC, an annual international symposium on urban issues. The 2008 symposium on global urban population growth drew attendance by more than fifty municipal leaders from the Middle East. Previous forums have addressed issues of globalization and sustainable infrastructure.

**Marty Kahn** is CEO of ProQuest, a company created in 2007 through the merger of two leading and historic information technology firms: ProQuest Information and Learning and CSA. ProQuest provides seamless access to and navigation of more than 125 billion digital pages of the world's scholarship, delivering it to the desktop and into the workflow of serious researchers in multiple fields. Mr. Kahn brings more than 30 years of experience in the information industry to his new role.

Mr. Kahn is a member of the board of directors and the finance committee of TrickleUp, a charitable organization that provides grants to entrepreneurs in the world's poorest countries. Mr. Kahn holds an MBA from Harvard Business School and a BA *cum laude* from Yale College.

**Julia Kent** has been a Program Manager in Best Practices at the Council of Graduate Schools since October 2008. She received her Ph.D. in British literature from Johns Hopkins and a Master's Degree in French literature from the Université de Paris VII, and is a former research fellow of the Ecole Normale Supérieure (Ulm). Before arriving at CGS, Julia was Assistant Professor of English at the American University of Beirut (AUB), where she served on the Executive Committee of the Center for American Studies and Research, helping to develop an American Studies program and research center that draws visiting scholars from North America, Europe, and the Middle East. At CGS, Julia is working on the Graduate International Collaborations Project (GICP), an NSF-funded project focusing on the development and implementation of joint and dual degree programs and research exchanges, and on the Project for Scholarly Integrity (PSI). She is also the editor of this issue of the Strategic Leaders Global Summit series.

**Maxwell King** is internationally recognized as a distinguished researcher in the field of econometrics. He has been a professor at Monash University since 1986. He is currently Pro Vice-Chancellor (Research and Research Training) and was appointed as a Sir John Monash Distinguished professor in 2003. He was head of the department of Econometrics and Business Statistics from 1988 to 2000.

Professor King was made a Fellow of the Academy of Social Sciences in 1997 and a Fellow of the Journal of Econometrics in 1989. He has held visiting professorships at the University of Auckland and the University of California, San Diego. He is a founding member of the Australian Council of Deans and Directors of Graduate Studies and is currently the Council's Convenor.

Despite a significant administrative load, he remains an active researcher having published over 100 journal articles. He has supervised 40 Ph.D. students to completion and received the Vice-Chancellor's award for postgraduate supervision in 1996.

**Christine Keitel-Kreidt** is Professor of Mathematics Education at the Free University of Berlin. Recently she was appointed Commissioner of the Free University for cultivating contacts and collaboration with the Australia Centre Berlin, as well as for organizing partnerships and exchange programmes with the universities in Melbourne, Australia. She has been involved in several comparative studies as investigator, consultant and coordinator. Her work on the history and current state of mathematics education in various European and Non-European countries, in particular in the USA, the former USSR, China, Indonesia, Japan, and South Africa, has been widely recognized. In 1999, she received an Honorary Doctorate in Sciences (Dr.h.c.sc.) from the University of Southampton/ UK and the Alexander-von-Humboldt/South-African-Scholarship Award for research undertaken in South Africa. She has been involved in many research associations and journal editorial boards in a variety of roles, including European Editor of the "Journal for Curriculum Studies" (1994-2000), Convenor of the International Organization of Women in Mathematics Education (IOWME), (1992-1996), and President of the Commission Internationale pour L'Etude et l'Amélioration de l'Enseignement des Mathématiques (CIEAEM) since 1996. Her research areas include studies on the relationship between mathematics and its social practice, on mathematical modelling, on attitudes and beliefs of teachers and students, on "mathematical literacy" and "numeracy," on equity and social justice, on learners' perspectives on classroom practice, and on the challenges of internationalization and globalization for mathematics education. Christine Keitel is one of the chief investigators of the Learner's Perspective Study.

**Karen Klomparens** has served as Dean of the Graduate School and Associate Provost for Graduate Education at Michigan State University since 1997. She is a Professor of Plant Biology and is on leave as Director of MSU's Center for Advanced Microscopy. With her graduate students, Dr. Klomparens published 60 peer-reviewed articles on the topic of ultrastructural development of sporulating structures in fungi and 3 books on electron microscopy in the biological sciences. Prior to becoming Assistant Dean for Graduate Student Welfare in 1994, Dr. Klomparens was on a Fulbright-supported sabbatical at the University of Cambridge. Her passions as a graduate dean focus on completion issues for doctoral students, diversity in graduate education, responsible conduct of research training and the educational environment, and facilitating interdisciplinary graduate education. She and her colleagues developed a FIPSE (U.S. Department of Education) and Hewlett Foundation supported program on "Setting Expectations and Resolving Conflicts in Graduate Education" that is the topic of a CGS monograph. The program uses interest-based approaches to resolving conflicts and has been used in a variety of settings inside and outside of academe for the past 10 years. Dean Klomparens served a 2-year term as the Chair of the Big Ten (CIC) graduate deans group and is currently on the Executive Committee and Board of Directors for the Council of Graduate Schools, the Executive Committee of the Association of Graduate Schools (AAU) and is completing a 3 year term on the GRE Board.

**Greg Koski**, PhD, MD, CPI is currently Senior Scientist of the Institute for Health Policy at the Massachusetts General Hospital and Associate Professor of Anesthesia at Harvard Medical School. Dr. Koski is an internationally recognized leader in human research and protection of human subjects. In 2003, he returned to Harvard after an extended leave of absence during which he served as the founding director of the federal Office for Human Research Protections (OHRP) at the US Department of Health and Human Services, Chair of the Human Subjects Research Subcommittee of the National Science and Technology Council's Committee on Science, and Executive Secretary of the National Human Research Protections Advisory Committee.

Dr. Koski was formerly the Director of Human Research Affairs at the Massachusetts General Hospital and Partners HealthCare System in Boston, a research-based integrated healthcare system affiliated with the Harvard Medical School. In addition to his clinical, teaching and research activities, Dr. Koski served two terms on the boards of trustees of the Association of Clinical Research Professionals and is currently President and Chairman of the Board of its Academy of Pharmaceutical Physicians and Investigators.

Dr. Koski chairs the Ethics Advisory Board of the National Heart Lung and Blood Institute's renowned Framingham Heart Study and chairs the Advisory Board of the Strategic Initiative for Developing Capacity for Ethical Review based at the World Health Organization. In addition to serving on numerous editorial advisory boards, he is Associate Editor of the Journal for Empirical Research on Human Research Ethics, a publication devoted to promoting evidence-based ethical decision-making in research involving human subjects.

**Xiao-ling Liao** is originally a scholar of Communication and Computer Science, and gave lectures on her specialty subjects for five years before transferring her attention to the management and development of higher education within universities. Approximately nine years ago, Dr. Liao was made director of the government-founded postgraduate organization, Association of Chinese Graduate Schools, and has been in charge of the organization ever since.

**Isaac Mazonde** is Associate Professor of Human Geography and Director of Research and Development at the University of Botswana, where he has worked since 1978, when he joined as a Staff Development Fellow in the former National Institute of Development Research and Documentation. His research interests include social organization for economic production, minority groups, technology transfer, food security, and research management. He is the author of *Ranching and Enterprise in Eastern Botswana* and co-editor of *The Operation of Multilateral Trade Organisations—Towards a Policy on Agricultural Trade within SADC: Focus on Botswana.*

**Bryan D. Noe** is Dean of the Graduate School, University of Alabama at Birmingham (UAB). He holds degrees from Goshen College (BA), West Virginia University (MA) and the University of Minnesota (PhD). After postdoctoral training in cell biology, he joined the faculty of the Department of Anatomy (now Cell Biology) in the School of Medicine (SOM) at Emory University and attained the rank of Full Professor in 1983. Noe's research interests centered on posttranslational processing of peptide hormone precursors. He is author or co-author of numerous papers in the peer reviewed literature, and of book chapters and invited monographs in this field of research.

Noe has had a long-standing commitment to graduate education. While at Emory, in addition to mentoring predoctoral and postdoctoral trainees in his own laboratory, Noe held numerous administrative positions that had an impact on the education of predoctoral and postdoctoral trainees. He was Associate Director of an NIH postdoctoral training grant in endocrinology, Associate Director of a predoctoral training program in Cell Biology, Director of Graduate Studies for his home department from 1977 to 1991, and he served as Director of the Graduate Division of Biological and Biomedical Sciences from 1991 to 2003. Noe also served as Vice Chair and Interim Chair of his home department, as Assistant Dean for Graduate Education in the SOM, as Associate Dean for Research in the Graduate School, and Interim Dean of the Graduate School at Emory.

On November 1, 2005 Noe assumed the position of Dean of the Graduate School at UAB. Since that time, Noe and the Graduate School staff have mounted numerous new initiatives which are designed to have a positive impact on graduate education.

**Suzanne Ortega** was appointed as the Executive Vice President and Provost of the University of New Mexico in August 2008. Prior to her appointment at the University of New Mexico, she served for three years as Vice Provost and Graduate Dean at the University of Washington. Dr. Ortega's masters and doctoral degrees in sociology were completed at Vanderbilt University. She served as assistant/associate graduate dean from 1994-2000 at the University of Nebraska and as Vice Provost for Advanced Studies and Dean of the Graduate School at the University of Missouri from 2000-2005.

With primary research interests in mental health epidemiology, health services, and race and ethnic relations, Dr. Ortega is the author or co-author of numerous journal articles, book chapters, and an introductory sociology text, now in its 7th edition. An award winning teacher, she has served on a number of review panels for NSF and NIH and she has been the principal investigator or co-investigator on grants totaling more than $6 million in state and federal funds. Her work to secure funding for and develop successful Ronald E. McNair Post-baccalaureate Degree, Preparing Future Faculty, Ph.D. Completion, and Diversity Enhancement programs, including the CGS/Peterson's Award for Innovations in Promoting an Inclusive Graduate Community are among her most important administrative accomplishments. Dr. Ortega is active in her national disciplinary association, having served on the American Sociological Association (ASA) Advisory Board for Preparing Future Faculty, the ASA Executive Office and Budget committee and currently serving as a member of the Journal of Health and Social Behavior editorial board. In addition, she has served on the Executive Board of the NASULGC Council on Research Policy and Graduate Education and is a past-Chair of the Midwestern Association of Graduate Schools and Council of Graduate Schools' Boards. Dr. Ortega currently chairs the GRE Board, serves as a member of the National Academies of Science Committee on the Assessment of the Research Doctorate, and is a member of the National Science Foundation's Human Resources Expert Panel.

**Robyn Owens** is currently Pro Vice-Chancellor (Research and Research Training) at the University of Western Australia , where she has direct responsibility for academic and strategic leadership in all matters relating to Higher Degree by Research Training. She also serves as the executive of the national body of Deans and Directors of Graduate Schools and has taken a pro-active role in a number of national policy areas, including the doctoral examination process and the use of modern IT systems to enhance both the management of the programs and the student experience. In her current role, she also focuses on quality in research and research training and the ways in which quality can be assessed and measured.

Originally trained as a mathematician, Robyn has a DPhil in Mathematics from Oxford and a number of years experience working in France and the US. Prior to her current position, she was Head of the School of Computer Science and Software Engineering at the University of Western Australia. Her research in computer vision has focused on understanding the geometric clues available from images that allow for the understanding of shape, object recognition, and eventually the semantics of the image content.

**Eva J. Pell**, the John and Nancy Steimer Professor of Agricultural Sciences, was appointed Vice President for Research and Dean of the Graduate School at Penn State University in January 2000, after serving in an interim capacity from July 1, 1999 until that time. On May 12, 2006, the Board of Trustees approved her promotion to Senior Vice President for Research and Dean of the Graduate School. Joining the faculty in 1973, Dr. Pell held a joint appointment in the Environmental Resources Research Institute and Department of Plant Pathology at Penn State University. In 1991 she was named Distinguished Professor of Plant Pathology, and in 1995 was named the Steimer Professor of Agricultural Sciences. Dr. Pell served as chair of the Intercollege Graduate Degree Program in Plant Physiology. Dr. Pell earned a B.S. in biology from City College of the City University of New York in 1968, and a Ph.D. in Plant Biology from Rutgers University in 1972.

Dr. Pell's research focused on the impact of air pollutants on vegetation and her research spanned from the molecular to the ecophysiological. She was the recipient of grants totaling more than $7 million and has authored or co-authored over 100 publications. In 2003, she was elected as a Fellow of the American Association for the Advancement of Science (AAAS). Dr. Pell serves on numerous national committees and organizations. Dr. Pell was the 2003-2004 President of AAU's Association of Graduate Schools and chair of NASULGC's Council of Research Policy and Graduate Education from 2004-2005.

**Susan Pfeiffer** is Dean of Graduate Studies and Vice-Provost, Graduate Education (2004-2009), and Professor in the Department of Anthropology, University of Toronto. As Dean of SGS, she is responsible for institutional oversight of all graduate programs at U of T, in which over 13,000 graduate students are enrolled in about 170 programs. Other institutional responsibilities include adjudication roles regarding appointments and oversight of the postdoctoral fellows office. She serves on the executive committees of the Ontario Council for Graduate Studies (OCGS) and the Board of the Canadian Association for Graduate Studies (CAGS). She is a member of the Research Council of the Canadian Institute for Advanced Research (CIFAR), and serves on an NSERC panel to review research grant structures. Previous administrative positions include Associate Dean and Acting Dean of Graduate Studies at the University of Guelph (1992-97), Acting Chair of Anthropology (2002), and Vice-Dean for Graduate Education and Research (2003-04) in the Faculty of Arts & Science at University of Toronto. She holds degrees from University of Iowa (Religion, B.A.1968) and University of Toronto (Anthropology, Ph.D. 1976). Her research in biological anthropology focuses on the reconstruction of past human adaptations, through analysis of the human skeleton. A member of Phi Beta Kappa and Sigma Xi honorary societies, she is an honorary research associate of the Department of Archaeology at the University of Cape Town. She has served as research advisor to over 40 graduate students and has received an Arts & Science award for outstanding teaching. She has published one authored and three edited books, plus over 75 book chapters and refereed journal articles.

**William B. Russel**, the A.W. Marks '19 Professor in the Department of Chemical Engineering, was appointed dean of the Graduate School at Princeton University in 2002. The Graduate School supports more than 2,300 graduate students pursuing masters and doctoral degrees in 39 departments and programs in all aspects of the endeavor - including both academic and student life responsibilities from recruiting through graduate alumni relations. He continues to pursue research that includes the crystallization of colloidal dispersions (akin to the formation of opals), theory and fabrication of micro-patterns in thin polymer films, and the drying and cracking of paint films. He is the author or coauthor of two books, the *Dynamics of Colloidal Systems* and *Colloidal Dispersions* and the Debye Lectures on *The Phase Behavior and Dynamics of Colloidal Dispersions.* After receiving his B.A. and M.Ch.E. degrees from Rice University and a Ph.D. from Stanford, he held a NATO Postdoctoral Fellowship in the Department of Applied Mathematics and Theoretical Physics at Cambridge University and joined the Princeton faculty in 1974. At Princeton he has served as chairman of the Department of Chemical Engineering and director of the Princeton Materials Institute. His 35 Ph.D. graduates now pursue careers in academia, industry, law, management consulting, and finance. Dean Russel is a member of the National Academy of Engineering and the American Academy of Arts and Sciences and serves on the executive committee of the AAU Association of Graduate Schools and as chair of the board of directors of the Council of Graduate Schools.

**Richard Russell** graduated from the University of Tasmania and subsequently obtained his PhD from the Research School of Chemistry at The Australian National University in Canberra. An author of some 170-research papers in Organic Chemistry, he holds a DSc and is a Fellow of the Royal Society of Chemistry and the Royal Australian Chemical Institute. He has held visiting faculty positions at Imperial College London and Texas A and M University. He has held two chairs of Chemistry in Australia, the most recent being at Deakin University in Victoria. During his time at Deakin he served as a Head of School and an Executive Dean of Faculty. Richard is presently Pro Vice-chancellor for research and Dean of Graduate Studies at the University of Adelaide in South Australia.

Apart from his research, Richard has been an enthusiastic teacher and has been awarded numerous teaching prizes including a prestigious Australian Award for University Teaching. In 2001 was made a Member of the Order of Australia for his contributions to Chemistry and Chemical Education. He has long held an interest in encouraging academic excellence at all levels and has lectured extensively to high school students around Australia. He was founder and, for a decade, director of the Australian Chemistry Olympiad as well as president of the 30th International Chemistry Olympiad held in Melbourne in 1998. He is presently Honorary Secretary to the Rhodes Scholarship Selection Committee of South Australia and regularly acts as a reviewer for teaching prizes and scholarships.

**Debra W. Stewart** became the fifth president of the Council of Graduate Schools in July, 2000. The Council of Graduate Schools is the leading U.S. organization dedicated to the improvement and advancement of graduate education. Its over 500 members award over 90% of all U.S. doctorates and approximately 75% of all U.S. master's degrees. CGS currently has 26 international universities among its membership. Prior to coming to the Council, Stewart was Vice Chancellor and Dean of the Graduate School at North Carolina State University. She also served as Interim Chancellor at UNC-Greensboro (1994) and as graduate dean and then vice provost (1988-1998) at N.C. State.

Stewart's service to graduate education includes chairing the Graduate Record Examination Board, the Council on Research Policy and Graduate Education, the Board of Directors of Oak Ridge Associated Universities, and the Board of Directors of the Council of Graduate Schools. She also served as vice chair of the ETS Board of Trustees, as Trustee of the Triangle Center for Advanced Studies, as a member the American Council on Education Board and several National Research Council committees and boards, as well as on advisory boards for the Carnegie Initiative on the Doctorate, the Responsive Ph.D. Project, and the Task Force on Immigration and America's Future.

Stewart received her Ph.D. in Political Science from University of North Carolina at Chapel Hill, her master's degree in government from the University of Maryland, and her B.A. from Marquette University, where she majored in philosophy. In November 2007, her leadership in graduate education was recognized by the Université Pierre et Marie Curie with an honorary doctorate. Her alma mater, the University of North Carolina Chapel Hill honored her in October 2008 with the Distinguished Alumna Award. She is the author or coauthor of numerous scholarly articles on administrative theory and public policy. Her disciplinary research focuses on ethics and managerial decision making. With sustained support from the National Science Foundation, she has conducted research on political attitudes and moral reasoning among public officials in Poland and Russia. Since coming to CGS she has built a powerful graduate education research capacity in the organization.

**Catharine R. Stimpson** is University Professor and Dean of the Graduate School of Arts and Science at New York University. From January, 1994 to October, 1997, she served as Director of the Fellows Program at the MacArthur Foundation in Chicago. Simultaneously, she was on leave from her position as University Professor at Rutgers, The State University of New Jersey-New Brunswick, where, from 1986-1992, she was also Dean of the Graduate School and Vice Provost for Graduate Education. Before going to Rutgers, she taught at Barnard College, where she was also the first director of its Women's Center. Now the editor of a book series for the University of Chicago Press, she was the founding editor of *Signs: Journal of Women in Culture and Society* from 1974-80.

The author of a novel, *Class Notes* (1979, 1980) and the editor of seven books, she has also published over 150 monographs, essays, stories, and reviews in such places as *Transatlantic Review, Nation, New York Times Book Review, Critical Inquiry*, and *boundary 2*. A selection of essays on literature, culture, and education, *Where The Meanings Are*, appeared in 1988. Her books on Gertrude Stein are under contract to the University of Chicago Press. She served as co-editor of the two-volume Library of America edition of the works of Gertrude Stein. Professor Stimpson has lectured at approximately 360 institutions and events in the United States and abroad.

Professor Stimpson's public service has included the chairpersonships of the New York State Council for the Humanities, the National Council for Research on Women, and the *Ms. Magazine* Board of Scholars. In 1990, she was the President of the Modern Language Association. She is now a member of the board of directors of several educational and cultural organizations, and a former member of the board of PBS. From September 2000 through September 2001, she served as the president of the Association of Graduate Schools. She is chair of the board of Creative Capital, the innovative arts organization. As a member of the Editorial Group of *Change* magazine from 1992 to 1994, she wrote a regular column about education and culture.

Born in Bellingham, Washington, Professor Stimpson was educated at Bryn Mawr College, Cambridge University, and Columbia University. She holds honorary degrees from Upsala College, Monmouth College, Bates College, Florida International University, the State University of New York at Albany, Hamilton College, the University of Arizona, Wheaton College, Hood College, Union College, Holy Cross College, Santa Clara University, and Rutgers University. She has also won Fulbright and Rockefeller Humanities Fellowships.

**Shi-Gang Sun** is Professor of Chemistry, Dean of the Graduate School, and Vice-President of Xiamen University. He received his Doctorat d'Etat in Physical Sciences from the University of Pierre et Marie Curie (Paris VI) and his B.S. in Chemistry from Xiamen University. He has been a Fellow of the International Society of Electrochemistry, a Fellow of the Royal Society of Chemistry (UK), a Council Member of the Chinese Chemical Society, a Member of the Standing Committee of Chinese Society of micro and nano technology, and Council member of the Chinese Society of Surface and Interface Physics. Dr. Sun's research interests include Surface Electrochemistry, Electrochemistry of Metallic Single Crystal Electrodes, Electrocatalysis, Electroanalysis, Electrochemistry of nanomaterials, Spectroelectrochemistry (IR), Kinetics of Electrochemical reactions, Organic electrochemistry, and Electrochemical power sources (Batteries, Fuel Cells).

**Lisa A. Tedesco** joined Emory in May 2006 as Vice Provost for Academic Affairs, Graduate Studies, and Dean of the Graduate School. She is a professor in the Rollins School of Public Health, Department of Behavioral Sciences and Health Education. For more than two decades, Dr. Tedesco has served in a number of academic leadership roles, including Vice President and Secretary of the University of Michigan (1998- 2005) and Interim Provost (2001). She has also served on an Institute of Medicine committee addressing institutional strategies for increasing US health care workforce diversity, and in 2005 was appointed to the Sullivan Alliance to Transform America's Health Professions. She has provided leadership in activities to promote gender equity in the sciences and engineering.

Dr. Tedesco's accomplishments include the following: fellow in the Academic Leadership Program sponsored by the Committee on Institutional Cooperation (Big Ten universities plus the University of Chicago), and a fellow in the Executive Leadership in Academic Medicine (ELAM) Program for Women (1996-1997); past President of the American Dental Education Association; honorary member of the American Dental Association (1995); recipient of the Distinguished Alumni Award from the State University of New York at Buffalo, Graduate School of Education (May of 1998); University of Michigan Sarah Goddard Power Award for distinguished leadership and sustained service on behalf of women (2002). Dr. Tedesco earned her doctorate in educational psychology from the State University of New York at Buffalo.

**Mandy Thomas** was appointed Pro Vice-Chancellor (Research) at the ANU in November 2006. In this role she is responsible for sponsored research, Higher

Degree Research, research integrity, and equity. She is also Chair of the ANU's Human Research Ethics Committee. Prior to her appointment at the ANU Mandy was the Australian Research Council's (ARC) Executive Director for the Humanities and Creative Arts, a position she held from 2004. At the ARC Mandy managed the largest competitive grants scheme, the Discovery Projects scheme, which funds basic research across all fields except clinical medical research.

Professor Thomas is a social anthropologist with extensive multi-disciplinary experience which has involved research, consultancies and publications in the areas of Indigenous Australia, multicultural Australia, and Asian studies.

**Prof. Anthony Yeh** is Chair Professor and Head of the Department of Urban Planning and Design, Dean of the Graduate School, and Director of the GIS Research Centre at the University of Hong Kong. He is an Academician of the Chinese Academy of Sciences and a Fellow of the Hong Kong Institute of Planners (HKIP), Royal Town Planning Institute (RTPI), Planning Institute of Australia (FPIA), British Computer Society (BCS) and the Chartered Institute of Logistics and Transport (CILT). He received the Hong Kong Croucher Foundation Senior Research Fellowships Award in 2001 and the UN-HABITAT Lecture Award in 2008.

Dr. Yeh's main areas of specialization are in urban development and planning in Hong Kong, China, and S.E. Asia and the applications of computers in urban and regional planning, particularly geographic information systems (GIS). He has done consultancy work related to his expertise in projects for the Hong Kong Government, World Bank, Canadian International Development Agency (CIDA), Urban Management Programme (UMP), and Asian Development Bank (ADB). He has served in various government consultation boards of the Hong Kong Government and is at present member of the Lands and Building Advisory Committee of the Hong Kong SAR Government.

At present, he is the Secretary-General of the Asian Planning Schools Association and Asia GIS Association. He has been the Chairman of the Hong Kong Geographical Association, Vice-President of the Commonwealth Association of Planners, Vice-President of the Hong Kong Institute of Planners, Chairman of the Geographic Information Science Commission of the International Geographic Union (IGU), and honorary professors and external examiners of a number of universities and research institutes in China and S.E. Asia. He is on the editorial boards of key international and Chinese journals and has published over 30 books and monographs and over 180 academic journal papers and book chapters. His current research is on city competition and development in China, pan-PRD regional cooperation, high-rise living environment, elderly adjustment to new towns, short-interval land use change detection using radar remote sensing and real time transport GIS.